Little Bighorn Battlefield

A History and Guide to The Battle of the Little Bighorn
by Robert M. Utley

Little Bighorn Battlefield National Monument
Montana

Produced by the
Division of Publications
National Park Service

U.S. Department of the Interior
Washington, D.C.

About This Book

The long, tragic history of Indian warfare in the American West reached its climax with the defeat of Lt. Col. George Armstrong Custer and his 7th Cavalry in Montana's valley of the Little Bighorn River on June 25, 1876. Although the Indians won the battle, they subsequently lost the war against the white man's efforts to end their independent way of life. The story of the battle and its consequences is told in the following pages by Robert M. Utley in a compelling narrative of an event that has excited the imagination and provoked controversy ever since it happened.

National Park Handbooks, compact introductions to the natural and historical places administered by the National Park Service, are designed to promote public understanding and enjoyment of the parks. Each handbook is intended to be informative reading and a useful guide to park features. More than 100 titles are in print. They are sold at parks and can be purchased by mail from the Superintendent of Documents, U.S. Government Printing Office, Washington, DC 20402.

Library of Congress Cataloging-in-Publication Data
Utley, Robert Marshall, 1929-
Little Bighorn Battlefield: a history and guide to the Battle of the Little Bighorn: Little Bighorn Battlefield National Monument, Montana/by Robert M. Utley; produced by the Division of Publications, National Park Service.
p.   cm.—(Handbook/Division of Publications, National Park Service; 132)
Originally published as: Custer Battlefield. 1988.
Includes index.
ISBN 0-912627-34-4
    1. Little Bighorn Battlefield National Monument (Mont.) 2. Little Bighorn, Battle of the, Mont., 1876.
3. Custer, George Armstrong, 1839-1876. I. United States. National Park Service. Division of Publications.
II. Title. III. Series: Handbook (United States. National Park Service. Division of Publications); 132.
E83.876.U792   1994   973.8'2—dc20   94-23568
                                                    CIP

Contents

Part 1

An American Legend

On a scorching June Sunday in 1876, hundreds of Indian warriors converged on a grassy ridge rising above the valley of Montana's Little Bighorn River. On the ridge five companies of United States cavalry, about 225 officers and troopers, fought desperately but hopelessly against many times their number. When the guns fell silent and the smoke and dust of battle lifted, no soldier survived.

This was "Custer's Last Battle"—a spectacular triumph for the American Indian in his four-century struggle to hold back the white people who finally overpowered him. It is an episode that has burned brightly in popular memory for generation after generation. Printing presses have poured forth a steady stream of books, pamphlets, and magazine and newspaper articles about the Battle of the Little Bighorn. Poets have found it irresistible. Painters and illustrators have turned out graphic representations ranging from giant canvases in oil to crude drawings on gum wrappers and bottle caps. Generations of children, and their parents, have sat in front of motion picture and television screens watching Indian warriors once again overwhelm the little band of cavalrymen and deal the mortal blow to "Yellow Hair." Today there are even national organizations devoted solely to the study of Custer and his last stand.

The Custer battle has also served as a bellwether of changing popular attitudes. In the first half of the 20th century, Custer was paraded through literature and across the movie screens as a conquering hero, symbol of the noble forces that opened the West to civilization and achieved America's continental destiny. In this scenario, the Indians served as mere impersonal foils, to be swept aside to make room for the industrious pioneers who followed behind the soldiers.

This drawing of Custer and the watercolor on pages 4-5 were done by Leonard Baskin, one of the seemingly infinite number of artists who have portrayed the events of June 25, 1876, and thereby contributed to the "American Legend" of George Armstrong Custer and the Battle of the Little Bighorn. The "foreboding air" that seems to hang over Baskin's drawings has been called a reflection of "man's mortality, brutality, and futility" in the face of tragedy no one seemed to comprehend.

Baskin
1968

Later, in the Vietnam years, Custer became a different kind of symbol. For more than a decade he personified all that was evil and brutal in America's historic treatment of the Indians and stood as a constant reminder of a deeply troubling guilt complex of the American people. "Custer died for your sins," proclaimed bumper stickers and the title of a best-selling plea for Indian rights. Custer and the Little Bighorn also became a metaphor for Vietnam. In the movie "Little Big Man," a lunatic Custer staggered about the battlefield roaring with mad laughter, underscoring the parallel that many people already perceived between Vietnam and the Indian Wars.

The Little Bighorn lives on in our imagination in part because of Custer himself. For 13 years he presented a hero-worshipping public with an irresistible combination: dashing, flamboyant, youthful war hero, and major general at 25; controversial explorer, hunter, plainsman, sportsman, author, and publicist of the West; Indian fighter, crusader against political corruption, personification of the U.S. cavalry, and ideal husband. Yet he was also an enigma, a man of bewildering contradictions, both despised and loved, ridiculed and idolized. All this, and dead on the Little Bighorn at 36.

The Little Bighorn lives on because people have found cavalrymen and Indians compelling subjects. The man on horseback has always ridden in the vanguard of our folk heroes, and in our image of the West the blueclad trooper and painted warrior have never been far behind the cowboy. And when these stereotypes are particularized, it is usually to Custer and his 7th Cavalry and the Sioux Indians of Sitting Bull and Crazy Horse.

The battle endures because the disaster to Custer's command, like the annihilation of the Texans at the Alamo, left no white survivor to tell the story. The rescue column found the unclad, mutilated bodies of the troopers scattered over the battlefield among the carcasses of their horses. The details of the fighting could only be guessed. The groundwork for endless speculation and debate had been laid.

For more than a century the full truth of what happened has eluded the assiduous quest of countless students. They have studied the documents and the battlefield itself, interviewed soldiers and Indians who were there, and pondered and argued over people and events. Today much is known about what happened and why. But many questions remain unanswered, and into the void has fallen such an accumulation of myth and legend that an entranced public has little hope of distinguishing truth from fiction.

Newsmen, Army officers, Indians, popular writers, historians, dramatists, poets, artists, TV and movie producers—all have contributed mightily to the legend of the Little Bighorn. For more than a century they have amassed a truly extraordinary body of literature and graphics. Still the presses roll and the cameras turn, the public buys, the controversy rages, and there is no consensus of what happened or why on that bleak Montana ridge in America's centennial summer.

Part 2

Custer's Last Battle

Road to the Little Bighorn

Lt. Col. George Armstrong Custer, who achieved glory and immortality at the Little Bighorn, is one of the most colorful and controversial figures in American history. This photograph of him in dress uniform was taken in New York in early 1876, just a few months before the Sioux campaign got underway. It was one of Mrs. Custer's favorite portraits. **Previous pages**: *The Battle of the Little Bighorn as seen by Sioux chief Red Horse.*

The Indians who wiped out Custer were Teton Sioux and Northern Cheyennes. Seven separate tribes made up the Teton Sioux—Hunkpapa, Blackfoot, Oglala, Brule, Two Kettle, Sans Arc, and Miniconjou. Once they had lived around the headwaters of the Mississippi River, but, pressed by Chippewas armed with muskets obtained from white traders, they retreated in the late 18th century westward to the Missouri River and beyond. In turn they pushed aside weaker tribes and finally overspread the plains cut by the valleys of the Yellowstone River and its major tributaries, the Powder, Tongue, and Bighorn.

The Cheyennes followed a similar course but migrated to the southwest and made their homes along the upper Platte River. Here they gradually split into two divisions. The Southern Cheyennes generally lived on the High Plains between the Platte and Arkansas Rivers. The Northern Cheyennes drifted northward to the country the Sioux now claimed.

This land, so bounteous in buffalo and other resources that supported the Plains Indians' way of life, belonged to the Crow tribe. The Sioux swept aside the Crows, thus touching off generations of conflict between the two peoples. In this warfare the Northern Cheyennes allied themselves with the Sioux.

Then another tide rolled westward, this one of white people. Like the Crows before them, the Tetons were confronted with a powerful threat to their territory and freedom. They felt the first tremors in the early 1860s, when gold discoveries in the mountains of Idaho and western Montana set off a rush to the new bonanzas. Gold seekers went up the Missouri River on steamboats or set out in wagon trains overland to the mountains.

The Indians resisted. Soldiers marched against them. Brig. Gen. Alfred Sully led an army of 2,000 to the Yellowstone in 1864, and Maj. Gen. Patrick E. Connor threw three strong columns into the Powder River country in 1865. Sully won a victory at Kill-

13

deer Mountain, but Connor's army almost disintegrated when his supply system broke down.

Recipe for Disaster

The end of the Civil War in 1865 gave new momentum to the westward movement of white Americans. Workmen pushed the rails of the Union Pacific up the Platte River Valley to meet and join in 1869 with the Central Pacific beyond the Rocky Mountains. The Northern Pacific built from St. Paul, Minnesota, aiming for Dakota Territory and ultimately the Pacific Northwest. Steamers continued to ply the Missouri, carrying passengers and freight to Fort Benton, the head of navigation, for the land journey to the gold mines. Along the railroad and steamboat routes the little postwar regular Army built forts and stationed troops to guard travelers and settlers.

For the Tetons and their Northern Cheyenne allies, the most serious menace loomed in the south. Beginning in 1866, emigrants increasingly looked to the Bozeman Trail as the best route to the Montana mines. Angling northwestward from the North Platte River, this route crossed the Powder, Tongue, and Bighorn Rivers, struck the Yellowstone on its upper reaches, and continued to Virginia City and other mining camps.

Piercing the Sioux buffalo ranges as it did, the trail infuriated the Indians, especially when soldiers came to protect it. Three guardian forts, Reno, Phil Kearny, and C.F. Smith, planted the Army in the midst of Sioux country. The tribes fought back, cutting off travel on the trail and bottling up the troops in their rude forts.

The Sioux had many fine leaders that year of 1866, but increasingly they gave allegiance to one who was not even a chief—Red Cloud. Skilled in war and politics, Red Cloud mobilized the Teton tribes against the hated forts. A mystical young warrior named Crazy Horse also rose to prominence. He played a critical role in the conflict by leading a decoy party that enticed 81 soldiers and civilians out of Fort Phil Kearny squarely into an ambush. All perished.

The annihilation of Capt. William J. Fetterman and his command on December 21, 1866, stunned the nation and prompted demands for vengeance. Even so, Red Cloud won the war. Despite setbacks at the Wagon Box and Hayfield fights in August

1867, the Indians effectively disrupted travel on the Bozeman Trail. The Government decided that the forts would have to be abandoned. For the Army it was a humiliating retreat. But for the gold seekers it made little difference: the rapid construction of the Union Pacific Railroad made the Montana mines more accessible by other routes.

The Government formalized its surrender in the Fort Laramie Treaty of 1868. Maddeningly, Red Cloud refused to sign until the soldiers had actually pulled out of the forts, after which his warriors promptly rode in and laid them waste. Even then, the Oglala leader tarried to hunt buffalo before finally journeying down to Fort Laramie, almost six months after he had been expected, to make his mark on the treaty.

The Treaty of 1868 laid the groundwork for endless trouble between the Indians and the United States Government. The Government's aim was to get the Sioux together where they could be watched and controlled. That meant setting aside a reservation and feeding them. The treaty therefore established all of present South Dakota west of the Missouri River as the Great Sioux Reservation. In this sweep of plains the Sioux would live while drawing rations and other provisions at agencies along the Missouri River.

But the Sioux had won the war, and not all wished to become agency Indians. Besides giving up the Bozeman Trail, therefore, the Government agreed to an "unceded territory," free of whites, stretching from the western boundary of the reservation to the summit of the Big Horn Mountains. Here in the Powder River Basin, long the heart of the Sioux domain, the Indians could continue to follow the buffalo.

Most of the Tetons, some 15,000, succumbed to the lure of free rations and went to the reservation. Even Red Cloud, after exasperating Government officials with shifting demands, finally gave in. But neither he nor his equally powerful rival, Spotted Tail, chief of the Brules, wanted an agency on the Missouri. The Indian Bureau at last agreed to locations far up the White River, across the reservation boundary in Nebraska, and established Red Cloud and Spotted Tail agencies. Other agencies, chief among them Cheyenne River and Grand River (re-

Centennial Summer

In 1876 the United States celebrated its centennial. President Ulysses S. Grant (*inset left*) launched a seven-month birthday party on May 10 in Philadelphia, where, a century earlier, delegates from the colonies had cut the ties with Great Britain. In Fairmount Park, in some 200 gaudy buildings, multitudes of visitors marveled at exhibits that recorded a hundred years of industrial and cultural progress.

The displays reflected the Nation's mood. Dominated by the huge Corliss steam engine, the array of machines and other examples of industrial might captured the exuberant self-congratulation that animated Americans at the onset of the Gilded Age. They also exhibited a bizarre taste that produced such wonders as a Liberty Bell fashioned from tobacco plugs and a likeness of George Washington made from the hair of Venezuelan patriot Simon Bolivar.

On July 3, Gens. William T. Sherman and Philip H. Sheridan joined thousands of other celebrants for festivities opening the Nation's 100th birthday. At midnight, fireworks burst over flag-draped Independence Hall to illumine throngs of patriotic revelers. Later, the generals toured the exposition. On July 6, along with all of Philadelphia, they opened the morning newspapers to read garbled accounts of a military disaster on the western frontier. Questioned by reporters, both generals ridiculed the news as a wild fantasy. At this moment, an aide handed Sherman a telegram. It confirmed the newspaper reports. Custer was dead.

Thousands of people from around the world throng the Centennial grounds in Philadelphia's Fairmount Park.

Red Cloud. When he signed the Fort Laramie treaty in November 1868, this powerful Oglala Sioux chief became the only Indian leader to win a war with the United States. He promised to try to keep his people out of future conflicts with the whites, but he had no control over younger warriors like Sitting Bull, Crazy Horse, and Gall, who resisted the U.S. Government's "civilizing" program under the provisions of the Laramie treaty.

named Standing Rock in 1875), rose from the banks of the Missouri River to the east.

Not all the Indians settled on the Great Sioux Reservation. A hard core of holdouts, about 3,000 Sioux and 400 Cheyennes, stubbornly resisted all overtures from the Government. They wanted nothing to do with white people or agencies or rations. They preferred the old life of the chase, and so long as the buffalo ran in the unceded territory they remained free to do as they pleased.

The Indians in the unceded territory followed their own tribal chiefs and noted warriors. The Hunkpapas, for example, boasted Black Moon, Four Horns, Gall, Crow King, and Rain-in-the-Face; the Miniconjous, Lame Deer and Hump; the Sans Arc, Black Eagle and Spotted Eagle; the Blackfoot Sioux, Jumping Bear (later known as John Grass); and the Oglalas, the incomparable Crazy Horse. Since his success in luring Captain Fetterman into the fatal trap set by his people in 1866, Crazy Horse, still the silent enigma of his early years, had emerged as the most powerful of the non-treaty Oglalas. The Northern Cheyennes, too, closely allied to the Sioux, counted dynamic leaders among their own roving bands: Dull Knife, Little Wolf, Two Moons, Dirty Moccasins, and Lame White Man.

Above all the tribal leaders, however, towered a single chief of commanding influence—Sitting Bull of the Hunkpapas. In earlier battles, especially the fighting against General Sully in 1864-65, he had made an outstanding record. Since then, he had broadened his influence into spiritual and political realms. Rocklike dedication to traditional Indian values and unwavering opposition to all relations with the white people ran deep in his makeup and fortified his dominance. On his tribesmen at the agencies he heaped scorn: "You are fools to make yourselves slaves to a piece of fat bacon, some hard-tack, and a little sugar and coffee." All the Teton and Cheyenne roamers, while honoring immediate tribal allegiances, looked beyond them to the forceful personality, superior intellect, and personal magnetism of Sitting Bull. In the eyes of Indians and whites alike, the Powder River bands came more and more to be identified as Sitting Bull's people.

These roving bands were a source of vast annoyance to the U.S. Government, for they offered haven to discontented agency Indians. In fact, many Sioux and Cheyennes shuttled back and forth between the Powder River country and the reservation, enjoying the best of both worlds—the old free life of the chase in the summer and the security and rations of the agency in the winter. On the reservation these people created endless turmoil, for they were unmanageable, a menace to agency officials, and a disruptive influence on their brethren who remained there year around. Off the reservation to the west, they did not always stay within the unceded territory. Sometimes war parties raided along the Platte and among the Montana settlements.

Government authorities looked forward to the time when the unceded territory could be done away with. None believed more ardently in the necessity of this move than the Army's two senior officers, Gen. William Tecumseh Sherman and Lt. Gen. Philip H. Sheridan. Sherman commanded the U.S. Army and, with seamed face, grizzled red beard, and caustic manner, radiated absolute authority. Sheridan, headquartered in Chicago, presided over the vast Military Division of the Missouri, which embraced the Great Plains from Mexico to Canada. A short, stocky, combative Irishman, he, too, ruled with iron hand. With Ulysses S. Grant, Sherman and Sheridan made up the trio of generals whom the nation credited with victory over the Confederacy in the Civil War. Now Grant was President of the United States, and his two lieutenants ran the Army.

Sherman, who had helped to negotiate the Treaty of 1868, never thought of the unceded territory as sacrosanct. "I suppose we must concede the Sioux the right to hunt from the Black Hills . . . to the Big Horn Mountains," he wrote to Sheridan in 1870, "but the ultimate title is regarded as surrendered." In fact, Sherman and other treaty commissioners had expected the problem to solve itself. As the buffalo disappeared, the Indians would be left with no choice except to go to the reservation. But this did not happen at once, and white pressure on the Sioux hunting grounds intensified faster than the buffalo diminished.

The first direct pressure came from the Northern Pacific Railway, which reached the Missouri River in 1873 and pointed its line toward the Yellowstone Valley. As he had with the Union Pacific, Sherman

looked to this railroad as the Army's strongest ally. "That Northern Pacific Road is going to give you a great deal of trouble," he warned Sheridan in 1872. But the Army ought to give every possible assistance, he urged, "as it will help to bring the Indian problem to a final solution." Military escorts accompanied railroad surveying parties into the Yellowstone country during the summers of 1871, 1872, and 1873. Although the Treaty of 1868 permitted railroads, Sitting Bull's warriors, in several armed clashes with the bluecoats, made clear their attitude toward this intrusion into their country.

Leading the cavalry component of the Northern Pacific Expedition of 1873 was a bold young officer already a national celebrity—Lt. Col. George Armstrong Custer. In life as later in death, this dashing cavalier provoked controversy. From associates he commanded either love or hate, rarely indifference. Some saw him as reckless, brutal, egotistical, selfish, unprincipled, and immature. Others looked upon him as upright, sincere, compassionate, honorable, tender, and above all fearless in battle and brilliant in leading men to victory.

A mediocre student at West Point, Custer had been commissioned a second lieutenant early in the Civil War. Within two years, at the age of 23, he donned the star of a brigadier general. From Gettysburg to Appomattox, the gold-bedecked "boy general" with long yellow hair and scarlet cravat led first the Michigan Cavalry Brigade and then the Third Cavalry Division from one triumph to another. War's end found him, at age 25, a major general and a national hero.

In 1865, after the great volunteer armies of the Union went home, the little postwar regular Army could no longer support all the generals who had conquered the Confederacy. Custer emerged from the war both as a major general of volunteers and a major general by brevet (an honorary distinction) in the regulars, but his line grade had advanced only to captain. With the reorganization of the regular Army in 1866, however, he won appointment as lieutenant colonel of the newly formed 7th Cavalry Regiment. Ever since, while the regiment's colonel remained on detached service, Custer had led the 7th in campaigns against the Plains Indians.

Custer's most celebrated victory came during the

war with the Southern Cheyennes of Kansas and the Indian Territory. On November 27, 1868, he launched a dawn attack on the sleeping camp of Chief Black Kettle on the Washita River. The troops inflicted a crushing defeat on this group but had to withdraw hastily when warriors from other villages appeared on the scene. The Battle of the Washita set off a lasting controversy. Humanitarians accused Custer of slaughtering peaceable Indians. (Actually, the chief was peaceable, but his young warriors had just returned from a raid on Kansas settlements.) Within the Army, and within his own regiment, Custer was both criticized and defended for pulling out and leaving behind a small part of his force later found to have been wiped out.

Custer and the 7th Cavalry came to the northern Plains in time to participate in the Yellowstone expedition of 1873. That autumn the regiment took station at Fort Abraham Lincoln, a fine new post on the west bank of the Missouri River across and downstream from the railhead town of Bismarck. Many wives joined their husbands, including Elizabeth Custer, a vivacious, beautiful woman, utterly devoted to her mate. She set the tone for a garrison life that was gay and briskly social.

Custer had got his first taste of the northern Indians in skirmishes with Sitting Bull's warriors on the Yellowstone. Now he would figure conspicuously in the next chapter of the gathering conflict with the Sioux.

Campaign of 1876

It was not the Yellowstone but the Black Hills that ignited the volatile mixture of Indian and white. The Black Hills were not part of the unceded territory but of the Great Sioux Reservation itself. With rumors of gold floating about the settlements of Dakota, the Territory's promoters, anxious to learn what the hazy blue mountains to the west might hide, agitated for an official exploration of the Black Hills. General Sheridan also wanted to know more about this area, for he had decided that he needed a fort somewhere near there to keep watch over the Sioux. Early in 1874, he won authority to send a military expedition to look for a suitable location. To command it, he turned to his young protege at Fort Lincoln.

*Elizabeth Bacon Custer was 34 when this photograph was taken in 1876. She was devoted to her husband and had followed him from one frontier station to another. Their last post was Fort Abraham Lincoln (**right, top**), Dakota Territory, which served as their home and Custer's base of operations from 1873 until 1876. It was from here on May 17, 1876, that he set out on the campaign that ended in defeat and death on the Little Bighorn. Mrs. Custer survived her husband by 57 years and spent every one of them guarding and perpetuating his memory. She died in 1933 at the age of 91. **Right, bottom**: Lt. Colonel and Mrs. Custer in the study of their home at Fort Lincoln, about 1873. The large portrait on the wall at left shows Custer in his Civil War garb; the one on the right is Gen. Philip Sheridan.*

For the troopers of Custer's 7th Cavalry, the Black Hills Expedition of 1874 turned out to be a summer's lark among forested, game-rich slopes drained by rushing creeks full of trout. On the northeastern edge of the Hills, Custer found an ideal site for Sheridan's military post (Fort Meade would be established there in 1878). But of vastly greater consequence, in the streams of the Hills themselves he found confirmation of the rumors of gold. A courier bearing official dispatches took the word out. "Gold in the Black Hills," shouted the newspaper headlines.

Even before year's end, gold seekers had rushed to the Black Hills, and the spring of 1875 saw the stampede under way in earnest. Custer City, Deadwood, and other mining camps sprang up in the most promising valleys. Vainly the Army tried to turn back the prospectors. Vainly, too, the Government tried to buy the Black Hills from the Sioux. Although some of the agency chiefs gave signs of weakening, the turbulent young warriors who spent part of the year with Sitting Bull would have none of it. Any chief who signed risked his life at the hands of these men.

The Indians' attitude irritated Government officials. Rationalizing that the Sioux had broken the treaty by raiding around the edges of the unceded territory, they laid plans to end the troublesome roaming of the non-treaty bands and to press the agency chiefs to sell the Black Hills. President Grant himself quietly approved a new policy. Soldiers would no longer bar settlers from the unceded territory west of the reservation boundary, "and if some go over the Boundary into the Black Hills," General Sherman understood, "the President and Interior Dept will wink at it for the present." These so-called "settlers," of course, were interested in the Black Hills, not the land to the west; the new policy meant simply that prospectors could now enter the Black Hills without military interference.

Shortly afterward, in December 1875, the Government moved against the "non-treaties." Native runners bore an ultimatum from the Commissioner of Indian Affairs to the Sioux and Cheyennes in the unceded territory: report at the agencies by January 31, 1876, or be branded hostile and driven in by the Army.

In their snowbound tipis the hunting bands re-

In contrast to treeless plains on all sides, the Black Hills held a special place in the affections of the Sioux. They treasured the Hills as their "Meat Pack," rich in game, with sheltered valleys and abundant fire wood, ideal for winter camping. Drawn by these resources, the Sioux had seized the Black Hills from the Kiowas a century earlier and had jealously guarded them against whites and other Indians ever since.

In the Treaty of 1868, the Government had included the Black Hills in the Great Sioux Reservation.

Whites coveted the Black Hills. Remote, mysterious, imperfectly known, the region inspired persistent rumors of gold that periodically set off mining boomlets in frontier towns. Settlers denounced the Treaty of 1868 and demanded that the Government investigate the reports of gold.

Officially, the Custer Expedition of 1874 sought a suitable location for a military post to keep watch on the Sioux. The presence of two "practical miners" with the expedition suggested another purpose as well. Their discovery of gold "from the grass roots down" set off a rush of prospectors.

The Sioux reacted in fury. "Thieves' Road," they branded Custer's trail to the Black Hills, and they angrily turned aside

Government efforts to buy the mineral region.

The Thieves' Road led not only to the Black Hills but ultimately to the Little Bighorn. If Custer dug his own grave in the Black Hills, as some suggested, his death on the Little Bighorn doomed Sioux hopes of keeping the Hills. In the atmosphere of national outrage stirred by Custer's Last Stand, the Government forced the Sioux to sell the Black Hills.

Top left: *Custer's two-mile-long wagon train entering Castle Creek Valley in the western part of the Black Hills.*
Bottom left: *The expedition's camp at Hiddenwood Creek, Dakota Territory, July, 8, 1874.*

Below: *Thirty-eight members of Custer's officer and scientific corps pose for a group portrait at the camp on Box Elder Creek, Dakota Territory, August 13, 1874. About half of the men shown here took part in the Battle of the Little Bighorn almost two years later.*

ceived the ultimatum with disdain. The deadline was impossibly close at hand, and moving camp in midwinter, especially such long distances, was exhausting and perilous. Such considerations, however, mattered little to the roamers because they had no intention of giving up their country or way of life for the reservation. Besides, they did not seriously believe that the Army would make war on them. They ignored the summons.

The deadline came without response. On February 1, 1876, the Secretary of the Interior, whose department included the Indian Bureau, certified all Indians in the unceded territory as hostile and asked the Secretary of War to take such measures as he thought appropriate.

General Sheridan welcomed this development. He had urged a winter campaign that would catch the Indians off guard and had fretted over the delay caused by the Indian Bureau's insistence on first giving them a chance to come in. At once Sheridan ordered his subordinate commanders to organize strong expeditions for an invasion of the Indian stronghold.

These officers were Brig. Gen. George Crook, commanding the Department of the Platte from Omaha, and Brig. Gen. Alfred H. Terry, commanding the Department of Dakota from St. Paul. Crook, a reticent, unpretentious man who rarely shared his thoughts or plans with even his closest aides, had come to his present command the year before after defeating the Apaches of Arizona. With a thick blond beard, forked and sometimes braided, a canvas suit, and durable mule, he projected an image of homespun simplicity. Terry, tall, bearded, and a man of marked kindliness and humility, had practiced law before the Civil War but had done so well as a wartime general of volunteers that he had been rewarded with a brigadier's commission in the regular service.

Sheridan drew up a plan that called for a strategy of convergence. Three columns, one from Crook's department and two from Terry's, would converge from three directions on the locale thought to be occupied by the Indians. No particular concert of action would be attempted, for each column would be strong enough to defeat any expected combination of Indians.

The Indian Bureau assured the Army that no more than 500 to 800 fighting men ranged the entire unceded territory, and they of course were scattered in their winter camps. This estimate, in fact, was close to accurate. Between 400 and 500 lodges sheltering a population of some 3,000 people made up Sitting Bull's following.

For the generals, the uncertainty lay not in the present but in the future strength of their opponents—in how many agency Indians would head west this year, and how soon. Thus Sheridan's anxiety to take the field before spring, when the yearly influx from the agencies would begin to reinforce the roamers.

But estimates of Indian strength figured critically in military calculations only in hindsight, after disaster demanded an explanation. No matter how many Indians gathered, the planners assumed, they could not remain together in large numbers for more than a few days. Their ponies quickly stripped the surrounding grass and fouled the water sources, their hunters decimated and frightened away nearby game, and their campfires consumed available fuel. As General Sheridan told a congressional committee in 1874, even though the Sioux might field 3,000 or 4,000 fighting men, "we cannot have any war with Indians because they cannot maintain five hundred men together for three days; they cannot feed them."

The fact is that no officer of the three columns doubted the ability of the troops to whip any number of Indians they could find. The great worry, rather, was that the troops would not be able to find them, or bring them to decisive battle if they did. Such was the lesson, with rare exceptions, of the Army's experience in Indian warfare.

Only one of Sheridan's three striking arms got under way before winter ended. General Crook, the "Gray Fox," organized a force of 800 infantry and cavalry at Fort Fetterman, Wyoming, on the North Platte River. Early in March he pushed northward on the old Bozeman Trail through deep snow and sub-zero cold. Scouts spotted an Indian camp on Powder River, and Crook sent Col. Joseph J. Reynolds and six companies of cavalry to attack it. On the bitterly cold morning of March 17, the troopers stormed into the village. The surprised Indians scattered but

Indian Leaders

The Sioux and Cheyennes had a number of outstanding leaders. Their authority over others, however, was much more apparent than real. In battle the Indian fought as an individual, not bound to any particular group and free to come and go as he chose. Indians did not have commanders and subcommanders as the U.S. Army did. Each tribe had various warrior societies, each with its chief and subchiefs. Some of them were great warriors, but in battle they could not give an order and expect to have it obeyed. Any influence the chiefs had was based on personal prowess, and they risked losing this prestige every time they failed in an undertaking. Some of the more prominent Indian leaders who took part in the Battle of the Little Bighorn are shown on the following pages.

4 Rain-in-the-Face
  Hunkpapa Sioux
5 Red Horse
  Miniconjou Sioux
6 Spotted Eagle
  Sans Arc Sioux
7 Low Dog
  Oglala Sioux
8 Two Moon
  Northern Cheyenne

29

Fort Peck Indian Agency

Fort Benton
1869–81

Fort Buford
1866–95

Fort Shaw
1867–81

Missouri River

MONTANA

Yellowstone River

TERRITORY

Helena

Conference on
the "Far West"
June 21, 1876

Little Missouri River

TERRY'S

Bozeman Trail

GIBBON'S COLUMN

Terry and Gibbon

Custer separates from Terry
June 22, 1876

Bozeman

Fort Ellis
1867–86
Gibbon leaves
April 1, 1876

Little Bighorn
River

Custer

River

Slim Buttes
September 9, 1876

Virginia City

Little Bighorn
June 25, 1876

Lame Deer
May 7, 1877

ROCKY

Hayfield
1867

Rosebud
Creek

Rosebud
June 17, 1876

Little Powder
River

Fort C. F. Smith
1866–68

Wolf
Mountain
January 8, 1877
Fetterman
1866

Powder River
March 17, 1876

Deadwood

June 19
1867
Wagon Box
1867

BIGHORN

CROOK'S COLUMN

BLACK
HILLS

Fort Phil Kearny
1866–68

MOUNTAINS

Bighorn River

Fort Reno
1865–68

Custer
City

IDAHO

Jackson
Hole

TERRITORY

Fort Hall
1870–83

Dull Knife
November 25, 1876

WYOMING

Oregon Trail

Wind River

TERRITORY

Fort Fetterman
1867–86
Crook leaves
May 29, 1876

South Pass

Sweetwater River

Independence Rock

North Platte River

Laramie
Peak

Red Cloud
Indian Agency

Register
Cliff

Fort Robinson
1874–1948

Fort Laramie
1849–90

LARAMIE

Oregon Trail/Bozeman T.

CENTRAL PACIFIC RAILROAD

Continental

MOUNTAINS

Scotts
Bluff

Promontory

Great Salt
Lake

UNION PACIFIC RAILROAD

Divide

Laramie River

Horse Creek

Lodgepole

Fort Bridger
1858–90

Cheyenne

Salt Lake City

UTAH

Green River

TERRITORY

South Platte River

Denver

COLORADO

TERRITORY

North

Pike's Peak

0   50   100 Kilometers

Site of
Bent's Fort

0   50   100 Miles

Colorado River

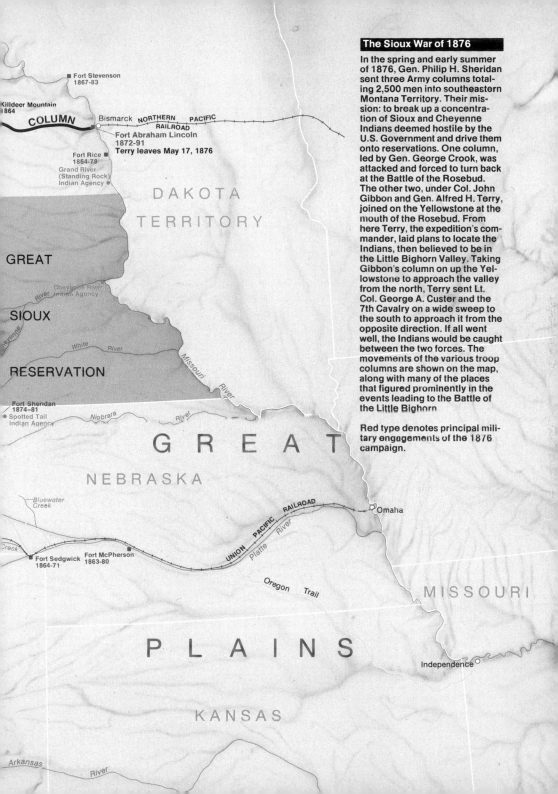

Fort Stevenson
1867-83

Killdeer Mountain
1864

COLUMN Bismarck NORTHERN PACIFIC
RAILROAD
Fort Abraham Lincoln
1872-91
Terry leaves May 17, 1876

Fort Rice
1864-78
Grand River
(Standing Rock)
Indian Agency

DAKOTA

TERRITORY

GREAT

Cheyenne River
Indian Agency

SIOUX

White River

RESERVATION

Fort Sheridan
1874-81
Spotted Tail
Indian Agency

Niobrara River

G R E A T

NEBRASKA

Bluewater
Creek

Omaha

UNION PACIFIC RAILROAD

Platte River

Fort Sedgwick Fort McPherson
1864-71 1863-80

Oregon Trail

M I S S O U R I

P L A I N S

Independence

KANSAS

Arkansas River

The Sioux War of 1876

In the spring and early summer of 1876, Gen. Philip H. Sheridan sent three Army columns totaling 2,500 men into southeastern Montana Territory. Their mission: to break up a concentration of Sioux and Cheyenne Indians deemed hostile by the U.S. Government and drive them onto reservations. One column, led by Gen. George Crook, was attacked and forced to turn back at the Battle of the Rosebud. The other two, under Col. John Gibbon and Gen. Alfred H. Terry, joined on the Yellowstone at the mouth of the Rosebud. From here Terry, the expedition's commander, laid plans to locate the Indians, then believed to be in the Little Bighorn Valley. Taking Gibbon's column on up the Yellowstone to approach the valley from the north, Terry sent Lt. Col. George A. Custer and the 7th Cavalry on a wide sweep to the south to approach it from the opposite direction. If all went well, the Indians would be caught between the two forces. The movements of the various troop columns are shown on the map, along with many of the places that figured prominently in the events leading to the Battle of the Little Bighorn

Red type denotes principal military engagements of the 1876 campaign.

Brig. Gen. George Crook, who commanded the Department of the Platte in 1876, had already helped to end Indian wars in southern Oregon, Idaho, northern California, and Arizona. He understood the Indian way of life probably better than any other Army officer and blamed most of the "troubles" on "tardy and broken faith on the part of the general government." His defeat at the Battle of the Rosebud on June 17, 1876, knocked his troops completely out of the campaign and may have contributed to Custer's defeat at the Little Bighorn.

rallied and counterattacked. Timidly, Reynolds abandoned his prize and fell back to the main column. Angry and discouraged, Crook turned about and headed for Fort Fetterman to outfit for another try. He did not march again until May 29, two months later.

Meantime, General Terry's preparations had been slowed by winter storms. Early in April, however, his "Montana Column" shoved off from Fort Ellis, in western Montana, and marched eastward down the Yellowstone River. Commanded by Col. John Gibbon, it consisted of about 450 men of the 2d Cavalry and 7th Infantry, with 25 Crow Indians, the bitter enemies of the Sioux, serving as scouts. On May 17 Terry's other force, the "Dakota Column," finally marched out of Fort Lincoln and pointed west toward the Yellowstone. Sheridan's winter campaign had become a summer campaign.

Terry himself commanded the Dakota Column. He had meant Custer to command. But during the spring Custer had been summoned to Washington as a witness in congressional hearings on frontier fraud. His testimony so angered President Grant that he ordered Terry to launch the expedition without Custer. Sheridan and Terry both asked the President to relent, and he finally allowed Custer to go along— but only at the head of his own regiment, and only under Terry's command.

The Dakota Column included all 12 companies of the 7th Cavalry. Numbering about 600 officers and troopers, the regiment stood at little more than half its authorized strength. In addition, there were two companies of the 17th Infantry and one of the 6th to guard a train of 150 supply wagons, a detachment of the 20th Infantry serving three rapid-fire Gatling guns, and about 35 Arikara Indian scouts. Altogether, the Dakota Column numbered about 925 officers and enlisted men. It was the 7th Cavalry, however, that Terry expected would run down the Indians and bring them to battle. Despite the President's displeasure, Terry believed the tireless and tenacious Custer just the officer to do it.

As customary, the Indians Crook and Terry sought had passed the winter widely dispersed in small camps among the valleys of the Powder River country and even as far east as the Black Hills. By March 1876, they had drifted to the Powder itself and its eastern tributaries. The village on Powder River that Colonel Reynolds attacked on March 17 consisted of about a hundred lodges of Oglalas, Miniconjous, and Cheyennes. After the soldiers withdrew, the warriors reclaimed their village and moved downstream, then over to the East Fork of the Little Powder to unite with Crazy Horse.

The fight on Powder River served unmistakable notice that the soldiers meant war. The combined bands now set forth to find Sitting Bull, who was camped about 60 miles farther north, on another branch of Powder River. Little by little, as word of the war sped from one camp to another, the Indians came together for self-defense. As the spring grass greened, they moved slowly westward from the Powder to the Tongue and on to the Rosebud, their numbers swelling as one group after another joined. By early June they had reached a strength of about 400 lodges—about 3,000 people, including some 800 warriors.

While camped on the lower Tongue River early in May, the Indians discovered soldiers on the north bank of the Yellowstone opposite the mouth of the Bighorn and sent in a raiding party of about 50 men which ran off the horses of the Crow scouts. Later in the month, after the troops had moved farther down the Yellowstone, warriors harassed scouting and hunting parties from the military camp.

After a buffalo hunt, the Indians moved up Rosebud Creek. Early in June they paused for a sun dance, the annual ceremony of tribal renewal and spiritual rededication. It was a deeply moving experience, made the more intense by the external menace and the common commitment to stand together in meeting it. In a prophetic vision, Sitting Bull saw many dead soldiers, "falling right into our camp." It was an immensely thrilling and promising image.

The spring grass not only fattened the ponies of these Indians but also set in motion the annual spring movement of their kinsmen from the agencies. From Standing Rock, Cheyenne River, Red Cloud, and Spotted Tail agencies, parties headed for the Powder River country. Besides the usual lure of a summer's hunt, this year they went in anger over the white people's attempt to seize the Black Hills and the Government's ultimatum to abandon the

Col. John Gibbon commanded the "Montana Column" out of Fort Ellis. A battle-scarred veteran of 34 years of military service, he was supposed to prevent the escape of the Indians that Custer's cavalry column would drive toward him. But he feared that Custer would find the Indians before his infantry was in position to block their northward flight. Gibbon's soldiers were the first to arrive at the Little Bighorn battlefield to rescue the survivors of Custer's command on June 27.

*Brig. Gen. Alfred H. Terry, Custer's commander, had headed the Department of Dakota since 1873. Though he had never led a field operation against Indians until the 1876 Sioux campaign, he was an able and well-liked officer. His ambiguously phrased June 22 orders to Custer (**opposite**) laid the basis for endless controversy over whether they had been obeyed or disobeyed. Terry refused all public comment on the subject, but privately he wrote Sheridan that "our plan must have been successful had it been carried out. . . ."*

unceded territory. And this year, because of these resentments, they went in larger numbers than ever. They moved slowly, waiting for the grass to ripen and their ponies to gain strength.

As Crook and Terry prepared to march, Colonel Gibbon tarried on the Yellowstone, his mission to prevent Indians from crossing the river and escaping to the north. Through late April and early May, he bivouacked on the north bank of the river opposite the mouth of the Bighorn, then moved downstream to new camps near the mouth of the Rosebud. Rain and mud limited his movements, but his Crow scouts, under the efficient Lt. James H. Bradley, kept watch on the valleys to the south.

Abundant signs gave notice of Sioux nearby, and the humiliating theft of the Crow scouts' ponies on May 3 erased any lingering doubt. On May 16 Bradley and a reconnoitering party spotted the main Sioux and Cheyenne camp in the Tongue River Valley, and Gibbon tried without success to get his command across the bank-full river to march against it. Again on May 27 the scouts located the quarry, this time in Rosebud Valley only 18 miles from Gibbon's position.

To the east, meantime, Terry and Custer searched for these same Indians. Curiously, in dispatches to Terry, Gibbon failed to inform his superior that he knew exactly the location of the big village that all three columns sought. Acting on reports that Sitting Bull himself waited on the Little Missouri to give battle, Terry sent Custer to scout this stream for signs of Sioux. Not until June 8, when he reached the Yellowstone at the mouth of the Powder and met officers from the Montana Column, did Terry learn where the Indians were.

Wrongly assuming the village would still be on the lower Rosebud, where Bradley had seen it two weeks earlier, Terry laid plans to trap it between Custer and Gibbon. First, however, he wanted to assure himself that the Indians had not doubled back to the east. He therefore sent six companies of the 7th Cavalry under Maj. Marcus A. Reno on a southward swing to examine the Powder and Tongue valleys and rejoin the main command at the mouth of the Tongue. He then prepared to push on to meet the Montana Column.

At the mouth of the Powder, Terry established a

supply depot manned by his own infantry and dismounted cavalry and another three infantry companies that had come upriver from Fort Buford. Here, too, he met Capt. Grant Marsh with the river steamer *Far West*, chartered by the Government to transport supplies and speed communication. Leaving all his wagons at the depot and organizing a mule packtrain to carry provisions, Terry had Custer march the balance of his regiment up the Yellowstone to the mouth of the Tongue. Terry himself steamed up on the *Far West*.

Major Reno violated his instructions. Finding no fresh indications of Indians in either the Powder or Tongue valleys, he decided to cross to the Rosebud. Here he promptly discovered recent campsites. Since Bradley's sighting of May 27, Sitting Bull and his people had not, as Terry supposed, remained in place but had moved on up the Rosebud to the southwest. Reno followed far enough to ensure that they had indeed left the area, then turned back to the Yellowstone to report to Terry.

Unknown to Reno as he countermarched on June 17, momentous events were taking place only 40 miles up this very valley. On May 29 General Crook had again marched forth on the old Bozeman Trail, leading more than a thousand men drawn from the 2d and 3rd Cavalry and the 4th and 9th Infantry. Near the head of the Tongue River he paused for a week awaiting the arrival of Crow and Shoshoni allies he had invited to help him fight the Sioux. When they finally appeared, 262 strong, the expedition moved.

On the morning of June 17, Crook's column halted for coffee on upper Rosebud Creek. Suddenly hundreds of Sioux and Cheyenne warriors burst upon them. Crook's Indian allies rushed to the attack and held back the assailants until the troops could organize for battle. For six hours the two sides fought valiantly among the rolling hills shouldering the Rosebud. In mid-afternoon the Indians broke off the battle and withdrew, leaving Crook bloodied but in possession of the field.

Burdened by wounded, the "Gray Fox" decided that he had no choice but to fall back to the base camp he had left only the day before. Also, the experience had left him badly shaken and determined not to risk another advance without a stronger

Terry's Orders To Custer

Camp at Mouth of
Rosebud River
Montana Territory
June 22, 1876

Colonel:

The Brigadier-General Commanding directs that, as soon as your regiment can be made ready for the march, you will proceed up the Rosebud in pursuit of the Indians whose trail was discovered by Major Reno a few days since. It is, of course, impossible to give you any definite instructions in regard to this movement, and were it not impossible to do so the Department Commander places too much confidence in your zeal, energy, and ability to wish to impose upon you precise orders which might hamper your action when nearly in contact with the enemy. He will, however, indicate to you his own views of what your action should be, and he desires that you should conform to them unless you shall see sufficient reason for departing from them. He thinks that you should proceed up the Rosebud until you ascertain definitely the direction in which the trail above spoken of leads. Should it be found (as it appears almost certain that it will be found) to turn towards the Little Horn, he thinks that you should still proceed southward, perhaps as far as the headwaters of the Tongue, and then turn toward the Little Horn, feeling constantly, however, to your left, so as to preclude the escape of the Indians to the south or southeast by passing around your left flank. The column of Colonel Gibbon is now in motion for the mouth of the Big Horn. As soon as it reaches that point it will cross the Yellowstone and move up at least as far as the forks of the Big and Little Horns. Of course its future movements must be controlled by circumstances as they arise, but it is hoped that the Indians, if upon the Little Horn, may be so nearly inclosed by the two columns that their escape will be impossible.

The Department Commander desires that on your way up the Rosebud you should thoroughly examine the upper part of Tullock's Creek, and that you should endeavor to send a scout through to Colonel Gibbon's column with the information of the result of your examination. The lower part of this creek will be examined by a detachment from Colonel Gibbon's command. The supply steamer will be pushed up the Big Horn as far as the forks if the river is found to be navigable for that distance, and the Department Commander, who will accompany the column of Colonel Gibbon, desires you to report to him there not later than the expiration of the time for which your troops are rationed, unless in the mean time you receive further orders.

Very respectfully
Your obedient servant,

E. W. Smith
Captain, 18th Infantry
Acting Assistant
Adjutant General

command. From his Goose Creek bivouac, near modern-day Sheridan, Wyoming, he called for reinforcements. Crook thus counted himself out of the events shaping up only a short distance to the north.

The intelligence that Major Reno brought back from the Rosebud forced Terry to revise his plan of action. Actually he changed the plan itself very little, merely shifting its place of execution farther west. On the morning of June 21, Terry penned a dispatch to General Sheridan telling of his new plan. Gibbon, he said, would march back up the Yellowstone, cross the river on the *Far West*, and then work his way up the Bighorn to the mouth of the Little Bighorn. At the same time, Custer would lead the 7th Cavalry up the Rosebud, cross to the upper Little Bighorn, and descend that stream toward Gibbon. "I only hope that one of the two columns will find the Indians," he concluded. "I go personally with Gibbon."

Terry's plan reflected both what he knew and what he did not know about his opponents. As for their strength, the campsites that Reno examined in the Rosebud Valley revealed about 400 lodges, the same as Bradley's estimate a month earlier. At two men per lodge, this made about 800 fighters. The whereabouts of the agency Indians, and whether any had joined the main camp since it had left the lower Rosebud, he did not know; nor does he seem to have worried much about it.

The Indians' location was also a mystery. Terry knew that about two weeks earlier they were ascending the Rosebud. They could have continued up that river or swung eastward toward the Black Hills, or they could have crossed to the Little Bighorn or turned north down Tullock's Creek toward the Yellowstone. The general impression was that they would be found on the upper Little Bighorn; lower down, they would be approaching the Bighorn, beyond which lay Crow country and the risk of a collision with their longtime enemies.

Because of the Indians' uncertain location, Terry's plan above all had to be flexible. Although not explicitly stated, everyone expected Custer, with his aggressive drive and more mobile column, to make the kill. Gibbon's role was mainly to block the northward flight of any Indians who got away from Custer's cavalry. Custer's mission, therefore, was to march up the Rosebud on the Indian trail. If it turned to the Little Bighorn, he was still to continue up the Rosebud before swinging west to the upper reaches of the Little Bighorn—this to make certain the Indians did not get away to the south or east and to give Gibbon's infantry time to get into blocking position at the mouth of the Little Bighorn. Terry expected him there by June 26, but this date had no other significance. The 7th Cavalry carried rations for 15 days, and Custer left no doubt that he would use them all, if necessary, to find the Indians. The notion that Terry meant for him to attack on June 26 arose only after the offensive ended in disaster.

That afternoon, June 21, Terry summoned his principal subordinates to a conference in the cabin of the *Far West*, moored to the bank of the Yellowstone at the mouth of the Rosebud. Bent over a map spread out on a table, Terry, Gibbon, Custer, and Maj. James Brisbin, Gibbon's cavalry chief, worked out the details and timing of Terry's strategy. In their talk they assumed, as usual, that the Indians would scatter and run if given the chance. (General Crook could have told them differently, but word of the Battle of the Rosebud had not yet reached the Yellowstone.) Thus everyone worried not about how to defeat the Indians but how to catch them before they discovered the soldiers and fled in all directions. As Gibbon said, the object of the plan was "to prevent the escape of the Indians, which was the idea pervading the minds of all of us."

The next morning, as the 7th Cavalry prepared to march, Terry handed Custer written orders that his adjutant general had put to paper during the night. In the never-ending, never-conclusive attempt to fix the blame for what happened afterward, every word and every nuance of those orders would be fiercely debated.

At noon on June 22, the 7th Cavalry passed in review before Terry, Gibbon, and Custer, astride their mounts. The regimental band, Custer's pride, had been left at the Powder River base, but massed trumpets provided a measure of panoply. Company by company, they trooped in front of their commanders, each raising its own cloud of dust, each marked by a swallow-tail guidon in the pattern of an American flag.

As usual in the field, the lean, bronzed troopers displayed every variety of costume. Slouch hats,

The Sioux Warrior

For Sioux males, war was both sport and ceremony, part of the very fabric of tribal life. It was a way to acquire property, especially horses, and to win glory and respect by performing brave deeds in combat.

The Sioux went to war to capture horses from their enemies and to protect and defend their hunting grounds. There were two types of forays: horse raids, in which the object was to steal into an enemy village and make off with its horses, and war parties, which were usually mounted for revenge or tribal defense. Horse raids might number from a few warriors to 15 or 20. War parties were usually larger, perhaps as many as a hundred warriors plus a few boys for menial chores and a few women for cooking. Before the advent of the white man on the plains in the 1830s, fighting between tribes was usually small and sporadic.

A warrior won honor in combat by "counting coup." A coup was an act of daring: striking an enemy, victory in hand-to-hand combat, saving a friend in battle, stealing a horse. It entitled a warrior to wear an eagle feather on the back of his head and distinctive marks on his clothing. Enough coups and a warrior had a war bonnet, which he wore in battle to show his ability.

A warrior usually went on

the warpath (if not into battle) with an impressive amount of gear: a bow and arrow, a knife, a shield, sometimes a lance, and a parfleche in which he carried extra moccasins, war paint, ceremonial items, a pipe and tobacco, war clothing (including a bonnet and coup feathers, if he had them), and jerky and pemmican. Warriors at the Little Bighorn also carried rifles.

Illustration by Richard Schlecht

The Cavalryman

The mounted trooper, unlike his adversary, fought for no great national or personal cause. He was a volunteer, often a recent immigrant, who did his job for his pay—about $13 a month—and the honor of his uniform. The Army taught him how to ride, how to use his weapons, how to fight, mounted or dismounted, with his troops or battalion, and it probably gave him whatever basic education he had.

It took the Army decades to learn how to fight the Indians on their own terms. The Plains warrior was a master of guerrilla warfare—skillful, highly motivated, and mobile. The Army was accustomed to fighting in conventional ways, which placed a premium on superior numbers and firepower. Eventually during the 1870s and 1880s the Army went over to mobile tactics, and by the use of better intelli-

gence, converging columns, and winter campaigning, it succeeded in breaking the last resistance of the Indians.

The cavalry was the main instrument of this warfare. When employed with infantry, it was a formidable opponent. This illustration shows a veteran cavalryman of 1876. He is dressed in the uniform that became generally available after 1873: a blue wool blouse, sky-blue trousers, gray shirt,

Items in inset illustration:

1 *Carbine and carbine sling*
2 *Saber*
3 *.45 Colt revolver and cartridge belt*
4 *Shelter half*
5 *Knife and sheath*
6 *Overcoat*
7 *Picket pin and lariat*
8 *Side line*
9 *Feedbag*
10 *Canteen*
11 *Haversack*
12 *Tin cup*
13 *Saddle bags*
14 *Poncho*
15 *Forage sack*

Illustrations by Richard Schlecht

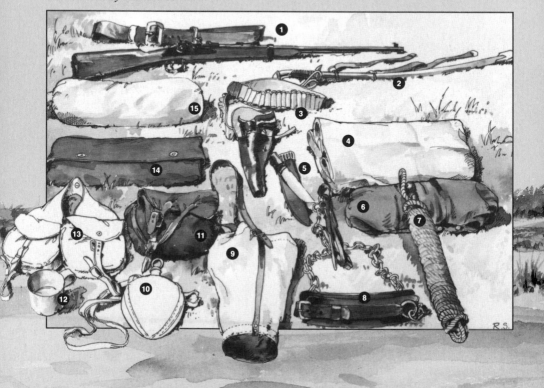

boots, and a broad-brimmed civilian hat in place of the Army hat, which was poorly made and quickly lost its shape. He is armed with a .45 caliber Springfield carbine (a single-shot breechloader) and a .45 Colt revolver, both models 1873. He was authorized a saber, but usually left it behind on campaign because he rarely got close enough to the enemy to use it.

*Custer's principal subordinates were Maj. Marcus A. Reno, **above**, and Capt. Frederick W. Benteen, **below**. While neither officer cared much for the other, they were linked first by their mutual dislike of Custer and then by the necessity of defending their conduct in the Battle of the Little Bighorn. Both men considered Custer highly overrated as a military leader and laid the blame for the defeat squarely on his shoulders.*

gray or blue shirts, and the regulation sky-blue trousers stuffed into cavalry boots predominated. To ease saddle wear, many had lined their trouser seats with canvas. Each man carried a Springfield single-shot carbine and a Colt revolver, with 100 cartridges for the former and 24 for the latter. Sabers had been left behind; they were cumbersome and soldiers rarely got close enough to Indians to use them anyway.

Custer's command numbered 31 officers and 566 enlisted men, 35 Indian scouts (the Arikaras, four Sioux, and six Crows borrowed from Gibbon), and about a dozen packers, guides, and other civilian employees. Bringing up the rear, a train of pack-mules bore rations and forage for 15 days together with reserve carbine ammunition of 50 rounds per man. The train had already begun to give trouble, some of the mules breaking formation and throwing their packs.

Despite his embarrassment over the train, Custer swelled with pride at the spectacle. He wore his customary field gear—fringed buckskin jacket and trousers, knee-high troop boots, the scarlet cravat and broad-collared blue shirt of Civil War memory, and a wide-brimmed white hat. Two holsters encased a pair of snub-nosed English revolvers. Close-cropped hair belied his Indian name, "Long Hair," and with ragged beard and fierce sunburn he hardly resembled the immaculate officer depicted by the artists of the eastern journals. A mounted orderly bore his personal pennant, displaying white crossed sabers against a red and blue field.

The regiment's formidable appearance concealed serious internal conflicts. Some of the officers accorded Custer blind loyalty and adulation. Notable among them were Capt. Thomas B. Weir, Lt. William W. Cooke (the Canadian-born regimental adjutant), and of course his own relatives: brother Capt. Thomas W. Custer, brother-in-law Lt. James Calhoun, and two civilians, brother Boston (hired as a forage master) and nephew Armstrong Reed (embarked on a summer's outing with his namesake uncle).

Other officers looked on Custer with contempt or even loathing. Among these were his two senior subordinates, Maj. Marcus A. Reno and Capt. Frederick W. Benteen. Reno, dark and swarthy, had done well as a colonel in the Civil War but no longer commanded much respect from his brother officers. Benteen, captain of Company H, had been a wartime lieutenant colonel. Lean, muscular, clean-shaven and white-haired, fearless in combat, he was widely admired as the ideal company commander. He returned the compliment with ill-tempered ridicule of all but a few brother officers. For Custer he harbored a passionate hatred that soured his character for the rest of his life.

Amid clouds of choking dust, Custer's troopers pushed up the Rosebud. They covered 12 miles that afternoon but racked up 30 each on the next two days. On the second day, June 23, they struck the Indian trail that Major Reno had already examined, and by the morning of the 24th they had reached the limit of Reno's reconnaissance. Here they paused at the site where the Sioux had staged their sun dance earlier in the month. The Indian scouts saw enough evidence of powerful medicine to make them restive.

Shortly after leaving the sun dance campsite, the column confronted another development. The Indian trail, hitherto by all indications several weeks old, suddenly turned fresh. Signs estimated to be no more than two days old suggested that the quarry could not be very far away, perhaps as near as 20 miles. The scouts probably knew the explanation, but no one consulted them and the officers speculated at length. Custer sent the Crows forward to gather more information.

Across the Rosebud divide to the west, circumstances conspired to give the Sioux and Cheyennes crucial advantages in the coming conflict. Ignorant as yet of Custer's approach, they had no plans to meet the danger he presented. Extraordinary good fortune, however, came to their support.

As Sitting Bull's following made its way slowly up the Rosebud through early June, a scattering of people arrived from the agencies. At the same time, however, others departed on hunting forays, to scout the enemy's movements, and even to trade for arms and ammunition at distant points on the Missouri River. The size of the village, therefore, remained about 400 tipis.

The scouting parties kept watch on General Crook as well as Colonel Gibbon. On June 9 one even tried to run off Crook's cavalry horses, but failed. On June 16 another group saw Crook break camp and head

Lt. William W. Cooke, 30-year-old Canadian soldier of fortune, was the 7th Cavalry's adjutant. He was a strong Custer supporter and one of the ablest and most efficient members of the regiment. He scribbled the last message from Custer on a page torn from his memorandum book and died beside his chief an hour later on what is now known as Custer Hill.

down the Rosebud. Hurrying back to warn of the danger, they found that the village had crossed from the Rosebud to a tributary of the Little Bighorn later named Reno Creek. The next day most of the young men, perhaps 500 to 700, rode back to the Rosebud and upstream to head off the soldiers, whose further advance would soon imperil the village. In fierce fighting they succeeded in their aim, for next day Crook's men countermarched to their base at Goose Creek.

The chiefs decided to move the village again. On June 18 the people struck camp, journeyed down Reno Creek to the Little Bighorn, then turned south, up the valley, and pitched their tipis. Here, a short distance above the mouth of Reno Creek, they remained for six days. Here they staged a festive celebration of the victory over the soldiers on the Rosebud. And here they gained another cause for celebration, for at last their brethren from the agencies began to arrive. On the backtrail from the Rosebud down Reno Creek, and down the Little Bighorn itself, they came suddenly and in great numbers.

During these six days Sitting Bull's village more than doubled, from 400 to nearly 1,000 lodges, from 3,000 to nearly 7,000 people, from 800 to nearly 2,000 warriors. In six separate tribal circles they crowded the narrow valley. Hunkpapas, Oglalas, Miniconjous, Sans Arcs, Blackfoot, Two Kettles, Brules, and a scattering of Yanktonnais and Santees (Sioux, but not Tetons) made up the five Sioux circles, while 120 Cheyenne lodges rounded out the great array. Even a handful of Arapahoes cast their lot with their friends.

The tribal leaders had planned a movement farther up the Little Bighorn, to the upper portion of the valley (exactly where General Terry expected to find them). Scouts, however, brought word of antelope herds to the north and west, downstream. On June 24, therefore, they moved the village northward, back down the Little Bighorn in the direction from which they had come.

The new location afforded an appealing setting. The upper end of the camp, anchored by the Hunkpapa circle, lay about two miles below the mouth of Reno Creek. The rest of the tipis sprawled along the west bank of the river for nearly three miles downstream. On the west the level valley, ranging from one-half mile to a full mile in width, ended in low grassy hills and benches where the huge pony herd grazed. On the eastern edge of the valley the river, cold and bank-full with the spring runoff from the Big Horn Mountains, meandered among thickets of shady cottonwood trees. A series of ragged bluffs rose steeply from the east bank of the river to a height of some 300 feet. On the south the bluffs fell away to Reno Creek, on the north to a dry water-course later called Medicine Tail Coulee, which opened on the river across from the Miniconjou and Sans Arc circles. North of Medicine Tail the breaks rose in tumbled furrows to a long narrow ridge paralleling the valley opposite the lower end of the village, where the Oglalas and Northern Cheyennes camped. From here one could scan the entire village and beyond to the snow-mantled Big Horn Mountains low on the southwestern horizon.

Here on the banks of the pretty stream the Sioux called the Greasy Grass stretched a village of unusual size. Such numbers consumed immense quantities of game, forage, and firewood and so could not remain long in one place, or even together in one village. It had come together in this strength only in the few days preceding, and it could stay together for more than a few days or a week only through luck, frequent moves, and constant labor. White apologists, seeking to explain the disaster this coalition of tribes wrought, would later endow it with an immensity it never approached. Still, it was big by all standards of the time, and it was more than twice as big as any of the Army officers looking for it anticipated.

Furthermore, and of still greater portent, the village contained a people basking proudly in the fullness of tribal power. Contrary to the planning assumptions and the mindset of Army officers, the Indians had little inclination to avoid conflict. Their grievances united them in a determination to fight against those who would seize the Black Hills and send soldiers to force them out of the unceded territory guaranteed by the Treaty of 1868. Sitting Bull's sun dance prophecy and their victory at the Rosebud hardened their resolve. And all these measures of strength aside, they would, as always, fight tenaciously if the enemy threatened their women and children.

Such was the objective that George Armstrong Custer sought as the sun rose on that Sunday, June 25, 1876.

Custer Family Casualties

The Custer family lost five of its members in the Battle of the Little Bighorn: the three brothers, George, Thomas, and Boston; their nephew Harry Reed; and their brother-in-law, James Calhoun, who was married to their sister Margaret. Tom Custer, a two-time Medal of Honor winner, commanded Company C and died beside his older brother. Boston Custer, a civilian guide, and Harry Reed, who had come along expecting to see the 7th Cavalry win another quick victory, were killed nearby. And Lieutenant Calhoun, commanding Company L, perished with his troops on the hill that now bears his name.

1 Harry Armstrong "Autie" Reed
2 Lt. James Calhoun
3 Boston Custer
4 Capt. Thomas W. Custer

Battle of the Little Bighorn

The 7th Cavalry's noon meal stop on June 24 stretched into four hours as the new and troubling Indian sign preoccupied everyone. Scouts rode out in advance to gather more information. "The trail was now fresh," noted the expedition's itinerist, "and the whole valley scratched up by the trailing lodge poles." Probably worried that the sign meant that the village was breaking up and scattering, Custer apparently did not guess the true explanation: the old trail had suddenly become overlaid and confused by the recent trails left by numerous groups of agency Indians converging to unite with Sitting Bull.

At dusk the regiment camped for the night. At nine, after darkness had fallen, the Crows returned with new intelligence. Just ahead, they told Custer, the Indian trail veered to the west and climbed the divide between the Rosebud and the Little Bighorn. They had followed it to the summit but, facing the setting sun, had not been able to see anything beyond.

Custer did some hasty calculations and at once adjusted his plans. Now he knew that the Indians could not be on the Rosebud. Nor could they have doubled back to the Yellowstone. Neither could they be on the upper Little Bighorn, for the trail up the divide was too fresh to have allowed time to get that far. Thus they had to be on the lower Little Bighorn.

Swiftly Custer made a crucial decision. Calling his officers together over a flickering candle, he outlined a new plan. Instead of continuing up the Rosebud, he would follow the trail across the divide under cover of night, spend the next day resting the command and fixing the location of the Indian camp, then hit it with a dawn attack on June 26, the date appointed for Gibbon to reach the mouth of the Little Bighorn.

Rousted from bivouac about midnight, the troopers groped blindly forward in the darkness, marching another six miles up the rough, rocky valley of a small stream now named Davis Creek. At two a.m.,

**Varnum's Detachment
of Scouts**

*Scouts, both white and Indian,
played important roles in the
Sioux campaign of 1876.
White scouts, like Charley
Reynolds, were civilians
hired at a specified wage by
the U.S. Army Quartermaster
Department. Indian scouts,
on the other hand, were enlisted men, who though tech-
nically not soldiers, were considered to be officially part of
the Army. But Indian scouts,
unlike white soldiers, signed
on for indefinite periods and
served at the discretion of the*

*departmental commander.
The detachment of Indian
scouts enlisted for the 1876
campaign were mostly
Arikara, two of whom are
shown on the opposite page,
under the command of Lt.
Charles A. Varnum (above).
A handful of Crow scouts on
detached service from the 7th
Infantry accompanied the
troops to the Little Bighorn
and were nominally under
Varnum's command. The four
Crow scouts shown opposite
accompanied Custer's col-
umn on the day of the battle
but escaped death.*

still short of the summit, the weary horsemen halted. As day dawned, they made coffee, although the alkaline water made it all but undrinkable.

Riding about the command bareback, Custer paused at the cookfire of the Arikaras. Bloody Knife, half Sioux, half Arikara, was talking. Custer asked the interpreter what he said. "He says we'll find enough Sioux to keep us fighting two or three days." Custer smiled. "I guess we'll get through with them in one day," he observed.

Earlier, while the regiment marched in dusty blackness, Lt. Charles A. Varnum and several of the scouts under his command had climbed a high hill to the west, part of the divide between the Rosebud and Little Bighorn, known as the Crow's Nest. At dawn they scanned the wrinkled landscape rolling off to the Big Horn Mountains. Some 15 miles to the west, where a thread of green traced the course of the Little Bighorn, the Crows spotted smoke rising from the Sioux and Cheyenne village, and on the benchland beyond they picked out an undulating dark smudge that represented the pony herd. Varnum could not see the village. Nor could Custer when he climbed the peak in response to the lieuten-ant's summons. But he had no reason to doubt that the Crows had seen it. They placed it just where the direction and freshness of the trail indicated it should be.

Almost at once, however, word came that stirred new alarm. Two parties of Sioux were spotted in the vicinity of the breakfasting soldiers. All experience pointed to the certainty that these Indians would hasten to warn the village of the soldiers' approach. Then the gnawing fear that had ridden with the regi-ment all the way from Fort Lincoln would be realized: the village would break up and flee in all directions. And so Custer made a second crucial decision—to find the village and strike it as soon as possible.

For his decisions on the evening of June 24 and the morning of June 25, Custer has been both condemned and defended. His detractors, pointing to his burning pride in the 7th Cavalry and his reputation as an impetuous commander, have charged him with will-fully disobeying orders in a heedless race to win all the glory. He disregarded Terry's suggestion that he continue up the Rosebud beyond the point where the Indian trail left it, then rushed a command exhausted

1 Young Hawk
  Arikara
2 White-Man-Runs-Him
  Crow
3 Goes Ahead
  Crow
4 Curly
  Crow
5 Strikes Two
  Arikara
6 Hairy Moccasin
  Crow

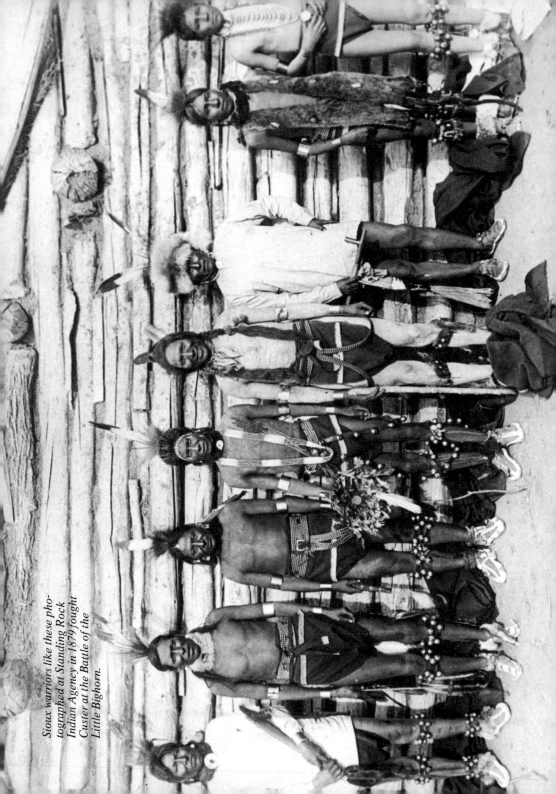

Sioux warriors like these photographed at Standing Rock Indian Agency in 1879 fought Custer at the Battle of the Little Bighorn.

Custer Divides His Command

Early on the morning of June 25, Custer viewed the distant Little Bighorn Valley from the Crow's Nest. Shortly past noon, on the divide between the Rosebud and Little Bighorn watershed, he formed the 7th Cavalry into battalions for the advance on the Indians, whose exact location was still not known. The route of the battalions to the Little Bighorn battlefield is shown on the map. The time at which each arrived at a particular point is approximate; it is, however, based on the best available information.

Crow's Nest

WOLF MOUNTAINS

Custer divides his command into three battalions
12:15

CUSTER

RENO

BENTEEN

Davis Creek

South Fork Reno Creek

Benteen joins Custer's trail
2:40

North Fork Reno Creek

Morass
1:50
1:50
2:50

Reno Creek

Lone Tipi
2:15
2:15
3:15

Lower Forks
Reno separates from Custer to charge Indian village
2:35
2:35
4:10

From this point Custer's movements are conjectural

Custer sees Indian village
3:05

In Medicine Tail Coulee
3:30

Calhoun Hill

CUSTER BATTLEFIELD

Custer engaged by
4:30

Weir Point

RENO-BENTEEN BATTLEFIELD

Benteen arrives
4:20

Reno's retreat; recrosses Little Bighorn
3:55

Reno on bluffs
4:00

Little Bighorn River

Reno fords the Little Bighorn
2:55

Valley Fight
3:00-3:50

Reno's attack on Indian Village stopped
3:10

INDIAN VILLAGE

Bighorn River

Little Bighorn

North

1 Kilometer
0   5

1 Mile
0   5

The scout Bloody Knife was the son of a Sioux father and an Arikara mother. He had served at Fort Lincoln in various scouting capacities ever since the fort was established and had taken part in a number of exploring expeditions, including Custer's 1874 Black Hills foray. Fearless and outspoken, he often ridiculed whites, including Custer himself. Bloody Knife's Sioux relatives despised him for fighting with the soldiers, and none of them mourned when he died in the valley during Reno's attack on June 25.

by a night march into battle without first learning the exact location and strength of the enemy.

Defenders point to the language in Terry's instructions leaving all movements to Custer's discretion. The Indian trail plainly disclosed that the Sioux and Cheyennes were so near that they could not possibly have slipped off to the southeast. To continue up the Rosebud would have required him to lose touch with an enemy he now had in his immediate front, to make a long detour through country he knew could not harbor many Indians, and to risk the very possibility that everyone so pervasively feared—the escape of the Indians. Once the regiment had been discovered, moreover, there could be no other proper decision than to attack, for the Indians could hardly have been expected to remain in place waiting until the soldiers found it convenient to fight.

Reno Attacks

Shortly after noon on June 25, 1876, the 7th Cavalry topped the divide and halted at the head of Reno Creek. Custer had his adjutant, Lieutenant Cooke, form the regiment into battalions. Major Reno took command of one, consisting of Companies A, G, and M—140 officers and enlisted men. Captain Benteen headed the second, consisting of Companies D, H, and K, about 125 strong. Custer himself retained five companies, about 225 horsemen, under his immediate command but subdivided them into two battalions. Capt. George Yates led the first, consisting of Companies E and F, and Capt. Myles W. Keogh the second, composed of Companies C, I, and L. Yates, a Custer loyalist, captained Company F, called the "band box troop" for its smart appearance. Keogh, captain of Company I, was an Irish soldier of fortune and veteran of the Papal Guards who had come to America in 1862 to fight for the Union. Capt. Thomas M. McDougall was assigned with B Company to guard the packtrain and bring up the rear.

Custer shared Terry's concern about the Indians slipping away to the southeast. What the scouts had seen from the Crow's Nest at dawn suggested that the village lay downstream from where he would strike the river, but prudence dictated that he make certain no Indians were upstream, where they would be behind him. From the head of Reno Creek, Custer could not see southeast into the Little Bighorn Valley; a line of ridges blocked the view. Immediately after dividing the regiment, therefore, he ordered Benteen to lead his battalion to these ridges and look for Indians before rejoining the trail of the main column. Subsequently, as Custer learned that more than one line of ridges intervened, he sent word for Benteen to move on to successive crests until he could see the Little Bighorn Valley.

As Benteen wheeled to the left, the rest of the column trotted down the narrow valley of Reno Creek. The two commands rode parallel, Custer's on the right bank of the creek, Reno's on the left. Lieutenant Varnum and the Indian scouts ranged in advance. The packtrain struggled along in the rear and quickly fell behind. A march of about ten miles brought the horsemen, by 2:15 p.m., to within four miles of the Little Bighorn. Here they rode through an abandoned Indian campsite. A lone tipi remained standing, containing the body of a slain warrior. The Indian scouts set it afire. (From the village at this site the warriors had ridden forth on June 16 to do battle with Crook.)

Here the troops flushed a party of Sioux. Interpreter Fred Gerard rode to the top of a knoll beside the trail, waved his hat, and shouted, "Here are your Indians, General, running like devils." Ahead, some 40 warriors raced their ponies toward the river. To the right, or north, Custer saw a column of dust rising from beyond high bluffs that hid the valley from view. The dust doubtless meant to him that he had at last found the village and that its occupants had taken alarm and were trying to get away. Even though Benteen could not be called upon, the situation demanded an immediate attack. Instantly, Custer ordered Reno to pursue the fleeing warriors, "and charge afterward, and you will be supported by the whole outfit."

Reno's battalion, accompanied by Varnum and the scouts, took up a fast trot down Reno Creek as the Indians vanished in the distance. At the tree-shaded ford the horses stopped to drink, throwing the formation into confusion. Reno finally got it reassembled on the other bank and led it onto the level valley floor.

Downstream in the distance, clouds of dust rose from the valley, and mounted Indians could be seen racing about. Gerard, the interpreter, concluded

that the warriors were riding forth to give battle. Knowing that Custer supposed them to be fleeing, he turned back to relay the news. Soon he overtook Adjutant Cooke and another officer who had accompanied Reno as far as the river. Explaining that the Indians were not running but were coming out to fight, Gerard wheeled to rejoin Reno.

Ironically, Custer had come close to surprising the Sioux and Cheyennes. They had only minutes of warning before the soldiers struck. Hunters were out looking for game. Except for a few ponies tethered in camp, the herd grazed on the bench to the west. Men lazed in their tipis. The soldiers, of course, also raised dust, and this first alerted the Indians. Warriors with ponies mounted, while others rushed toward the herd. The Hunkpapas and Blackfoot at the upper end of the camp made frantic preparations to meet Reno's advance and thus created the dust and commotion that misled Gerard and others.

With the three companies side by side in column of fours, Reno's battalion trotted down the valley. After a short distance Reno changed the formation, placing Company G in reserve behind M and A, then later brought G back on line with the other two. Ahead a timbered bend of the river jutted into the valley. From behind this tongue of green, dust continued to boil skyward. A few tipi tops could be indistinctly seen, and horsemen in growing numbers raced about in the dust. Anxiously, Reno looked back for the support Custer had promised but could see none. Another half-mile and the little handful of men would be swallowed by what looked like overpowering numbers of Indians, although probably no more than a couple of hundred had yet gathered. Reno threw up his hand and shouted for the command to fight on foot.

The advance ground to a halt within sight of the Hunkpapa circle. Pvt. James Turley's horse bolted and carried him forward into the dust. "That was the last I saw of him," said his sergeant. Every fourth man grabbed the reins of his own and three other horses and led them to the rear, then into the timber. A thin skirmish line stretched part way across the valley, carbines popping at blurred images in the dust. Mounted Sioux raced the length of the line, curled around the exposed left flank, and appeared in the rear.

The blue-and-gold regimental standard of the 7th Cavalry (**opposite top**) *remained with the pack train during the battle.* **Opposite bottom:** *Each of the 12 companies that fought at the Little Bighorn carried a silk stars-and-stripes guidon like this one to mark its position on the battlefield.*

Mitch Bouyer, half-blood interpreter for the regiment's Crow scouts, had predicted that there was going to be "a damned big fight." Both he and Bloody Knife warned Custer that the Little Bighorn Valley contained more Indians than the cavalry could handle. Bouyer died with Custer.

Within 15 minutes, Reno decided that the position had to be abandoned. His men filed to the right into the cottonwood groves that anchored the right flank. Here an old river bank afforded a natural breastwork, but here, also, dense timber and heavy undergrowth thwarted all attempts at a coherent formation. Reno quickly lost control of his companies. Warriors worked through the brush and trees and gathered on the other side of the river to fire from the rear.

Within half an hour, closely pressed, the major decided that this position could not be held either. He mounted and shouted for his men to mount. Scout Bloody Knife sat his horse next to Reno. A bullet sang through the trees and smashed into his skull, splattering Reno's face with blood and brains. Disconcerted, Reno ordered the men to dismount, then recovered and again shouted to mount. Confusion spread as some men obeyed, others misunderstood, and still others failed to see or hear their commander.

On the edge of the timber, the cavalrymen mounted in a loose column formation. Reno took the lead and signaled a withdrawal back up the valley. Sioux kneed their ponies in from the right. "When we came out of the woods," recalled Lieutenant Varnum, "there were a great many Indians scampering along with their rifles across the saddle, working their Winchesters on the column." This deadly fire deflected the retreat toward the river and the high bluffs beyond. No rearguard held back the Sioux, and soon they mixed with the galloping troopers, now seized by panic. "The Indians picked off the troops at will," commented Gerard; "it was a rout, not a charge."

At the river no force covered the crossing, and warriors gathered on the banks to fire at the soldiers struggling in the water. Those who reached the east side made their way up the ravines that cut into the rampart of bluffs. Exhausted and beaten, the remnant of the battalion gathered atop the bluffs. Of 140 men who had charged down the valley scarcely an hour earlier, 40 had been killed and 13 wounded. Among the dead were Lt. Donald McIntosh, cut down in the retreat; Lt. Benjamin H. Hodgson, knocked into the river, then fatally hit while being dragged up the bank grasping the stirrup of a passing rider; Dr. James M. DeWolf, dropped by a shot from the top of the bluffs while scaling an exposed hogback separating two ravines; civilian interpreter Isaiah Dorman, the only black man with the expedition, killed in the valley; and the noted scout "Lonesome" Charley Reynolds, also killed in the flight from the valley. Lt. Charles C. DeRudio and 16 men were missing. They had not heard the order to retreat and had been left behind in the timber.

No sooner had the broken command reached the new refuge than the Indians began to pull back. It was a stroke of timely good fortune for both the men on the bluffs and those in the timber below. But it was ill fortune for Custer, whose whereabouts Reno's men speculated upon as the Indians vanished from their front. It was now late afternoon, shortly after four o'clock.

Fred Gerard, civilian interpreter for the Arikara scouts, brought the first word to Custer that, contrary to expectations, the Indians were not running away but preparing to attack.

Custer Destroyed

Exactly how Custer and his men met their fate can never be fully and certainly known. None of the battalion survived to tell what happened. Indian participants gave confused and contradictory stories, at least to white ears. So, in fact, did Reno's men, especially as the enormity of the catastrophe and the search for blame began to warp their memories. These accounts, however, together with the placement of the bodies on the battlefield, provide a foundation for sketching the broad outlines of the action. More recent battlefield evidence, some obtained through archeological projects, has permitted further informed analysis. From these diverse sources the following sequence is deduced.

After Major Reno set off to charge the Indians in the valley, Custer and his battalion continued down Reno Creek to its junction with the north fork. While watering their horses there, Adjutant Cooke brought word as relayed by Gerard that the Indians were not running but coming out to meet Reno. If Custer had intended to follow Reno into battle, he now changed his mind, for he turned north, away from Reno Creek and toward the dust that continued to rise from behind the skyline to his right front.

Why? Did he plan to fall on the Indians' rear as Reno engaged their front? Or was he still obsessed with the fear that they would escape and took this means to block their route? Or both? Or some other plan? Or no particular plan at all? Although Bloody

Reno's Company Commanders
Companies A, B, D, G, K, and M, whose commanding officers are shown on the facing page, and Captain Benteen's Company H, took part in Reno's hilltop fight on June 25. Companies A, G, and M, totaling 131 men, were also in the attack on the Indian village that brought on the Battle of the Little Bighorn.

Knife and other scouts had tried to warn him of many more Indians than expected, he still knew no more of their strength and location than indicated by the dust cloud.

In parallel columns of twos, the five companies galloped up the long gentle slope toward the bluff tops. After a mile or so they halted short of the brow. Custer, his orderly trumpeter for the day, and the Crow scouts rode to the top and looked out over the valley. It was Custer's first view of the objective. Just below, the river swung in a wide loop halfway across the valley. "Down the valley," recalled one of the Crow scouts, "were camps and camps and camps. There was a big camp in a circle near the west hills." Below also, related another of the Crows, "we could see Reno fighting. He had crossed the creek. Everything was a scramble with lots of Sioux."

Back at the command, Custer conferred briefly with Adjutant Cooke and other officers, including his daredevil younger brother Tom, captain of Company C and the proud bearer of two Medals of Honor for Civil War heroism. As the march resumed, Tom Custer rode to his company and, motioning to Sgt. Daniel Kanipe, told him to hurry back to Captain McDougall with orders from Custer. "Tell McDougall," he instructed, "to bring the pack train straight across to high ground—if packs get loose don't stop to fix them, cut them off. Come quick. Big Indian camp."

As the sergeant turned aside, Custer resumed the march northward below the crest of the bluffs, although Varnum, fighting with Reno in the valley, glimpsed the gray horse company, E, passing along the skyline on the command's flank. Some of the horses became excited and broke into a gallop, out in front even of Custer. "Boys, hold your horses," Kanipe heard Custer shout, "there are plenty of them down there for us all." The command swung to the right, down a long north-trending ravine falling away from the heights. It was narrow and forced the formation into a column. After a half-mile or more, the ravine opened into the broad coulee now known as Medicine Tail. Custer signaled a left turn into the coulee.

Anxious to get Benteen into the fight and still worried about ammunition, Custer decided to send another courier. He motioned for his orderly trum-

1 Lt. Edward S. Godfrey
  Company K
2 Lt. Donald McIntosh
  Company G

3 Capt. Thomas M. McDougall
  Company B
4 Capt. Thomas H. French
  Company M
5 Capt. Thomas B. Weir
  Company D
6 Capt. Myles Moylan
  Company A

Custer's Company Commanders

The commanding officers of Companies E, F, and I, shown here, along with Capt. Thomas W. Custer of Company C and Lt. James Calhoun of Company L, were all killed with the Custer battalion on June 25. All were buried on the battlefield at the spots where they fell. Their bodies were exhumed in July 1877 for reburial elsewhere.

1 Capt. Myles W. Keogh
   Company I
2 Lt. Algernon E. Smith
   Company E
3 Capt. George W. Yates
   Company F

peter, an Italian immigrant who had recently angli-
cized his name from Giovanni Martini to John
Martin, and barked instructions. Cooke, no doubt
distrusting Martin's mastery of English, scrawled a
message on a page of his memorandum book, tore it
out, and handed it to him: "Benteen. Come on. Big
Village. Be Quick. Bring packs. W. W. Cooke. P.
bring pacs." The final words showed with what haste
Cooke wrote.

Spurring his horse up the backtrail, Martin glanced
over his shoulder. "The last I saw of the command
they were going down into the ravine [Medicine
Tail]. The gray horse troop was in the center and
they were galloping." Later he heard firing, looked
about, and "saw Indians, some waving buffalo robes
and some shooting." Farther up the trail, Martin met
Boston Custer hurrying from his post with the packtrain to join his brothers in the battle.

What happened next is reasonably well established by battlefield finds and Indian testimony. Why
it happened can only be theorized. The two-company
battalion under Captain Yates descended Medicine
Tail Coulee to the Little Bighorn River, while the
three-company battalion of Captain Keogh ascended
the north slope of Medicine Tail just beyond the
mouth of the ravine the column had followed from
the heights.

At the river Yates ran into a hot fire from warriors
posted in the brush on the other side. The bullets
flew so thickly, recalled a Sioux participant, "that
the head of his command reeled back toward the
bluffs after losing several men who tumbled into the
water." The Crow scouts, previously released by
Custer, watched from the steep hillside to the south
as these soldiers splashed into the water. Sitting Bull
later described this action succinctly: "Our young
men rained lead across the river and drove the white
braves back."

At first, only a handful of warriors, perhaps 30,
held the ford against Yates. But they quickly received help as men returned from the pony herd
with their mounts, and others, freed by Reno's
retreat, reached the new scene of action. The Hunkpapa Gall rallied the forces and led them in a rush
across the river. Back from the river Yates' companies withdrew, returning a ragged defensive fire as
they rode, dismounting skirmishers to hold back the

*Trumpeter John Martin, the last surviving trooper to see the Custer battalion alive. He carried Custer's last message (**opposite page**) to Captain Benteen, written by Custer's adjutant, Lt. William W. Cooke. Benteen's "translation" of Cooke's hastily scrawled summons appears at the top. **Below**: Sgt. Daniel Kanipe, who belonged to Capt. Tom Custer's C Company, carried the first message from Custer to Captain McDougall ordering up the pack train.*

Indian advance. These soldiers "held their horses' reins on one arm while they were shooting," remembered Low Dog, "but the horses were so frightened that they pulled the men all around, and a great many of their shots went up in the air and did us no harm." The line of this fighting retreat lay up the northern slope of a branch of Medicine Tail now known as Deep Coulee and ended on a low, flat hill forming the southern nose of a high ridge since called Battle Ridge.

The rush of Gall's warriors also hit Keogh's three companies, posted in strong positions on the ridges separating Medicine Tail and Deep Coulees. From dismounted skirmish lines, the troopers laid down a heavy fire, including some volley firing, that kept the Indians at bay. After 30 to 45 minutes, they withdrew.

Gall's warriors pressed closely. After crossing Deep Coulee, Keogh started up the south slope of Battle Ridge. Again, to relieve the threat to his rear, he dismounted and formed a line. Here, though, the Indians fired into the horse-holders and succeeded in felling enough men and stampeding enough horses to put the command largely on foot. With the horses went reserve carbine ammunition. "After this," related Gall, "the soldiers threw aside their guns [carbines] and fought with little guns [pistols]." Dismounted, Keogh's companies moved to the southern end of Battle Ridge and at last linked up with Yates on the hill that later took the name of the L Company commander, Lt. James Calhoun.

What Custer intended, or indeed whether he accompanied Yates or Keogh, is conjecture. Some students even believe that he fell, killed or wounded, with Yates at the river and was carried to the hill where his body was later found. Yates may have been the leading element of a charge into the village, with Keogh prevented from following by Gall's powerful warrior force. Or Keogh may have been working his way northward to strike the village from still another direction. One of several plausible theories is that Custer, delaying a decisive thrust until Benteen arrived with the packs, sent Yates to hold the ford and himself remained with Keogh on the heights commanding the route by which Benteen would come. Whatever the intent, the Indians proved too strong, and all five companies reunited on Calhoun Hill.

Benteen.
Come on. Big Village.
Be quick. Bring Packs.
P.S. Bring Packs.
W. W. Cooke.

Benteen

Come on Big

Village be quick

bring pack

W. W. Cooke

+ bring pack

This painting shows the Little Bighorn battlefield in 1876 and the Custer portion of that same battlefield today. Battle movements and the depiction of the Indian village are based on the most reliable historical accounts as well as the location of artifacts found by collectors and archeologists over the years.

58 Marble markers

48 Marble markers

Calhoun Hill

Battlefield Road

CAPT. M.W. KEOGH'S COMPANY

LT. J. CALHOUN'S COMPANY

CAPT.G.W.YATES' COMPANY

Last Stand Hill

LT. COL. G.A. CUSTER'S LAST POSITION

Visitor Center

CAPT. T.W. CUSTER'S COMPANY

LT. A.E. SMITH'S COMPANY

Deep Ravine

Little Bighorn Battlefield National Monument Boundary

Little Bighorn River (present course)

Nye-Cartwright Ridge

Deep Coulee

Medicine Tail Coulee

CUSTER

Calhoun Hill

GALL

Last Stand Hill

Deep Ravine

Little Bighorn River (old course)

CRAZY HORSE

Scale varies in this perspective view. Last Stand Hill to Reno Hill is approximately four miles.

© National Geographic Society

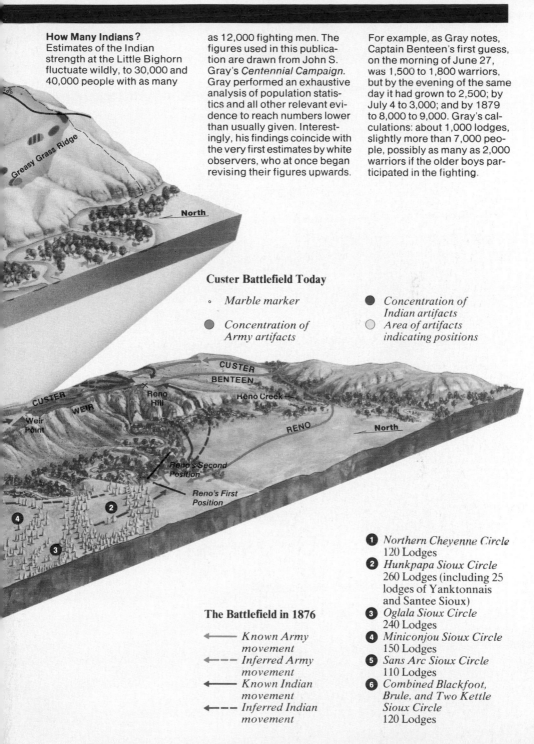

How Many Indians?

Estimates of the Indian strength at the Little Bighorn fluctuate wildly, to 30,000 and 40,000 people with as many as 12,000 fighting men. The figures used in this publication are drawn from John S. Gray's *Centennial Campaign*. Gray performed an exhaustive analysis of population statistics and all other relevant evidence to reach numbers lower than usually given. Interestingly, his findings coincide with the very first estimates by white observers, who at once began revising their figures upwards.

For example, as Gray notes, Captain Benteen's first guess, on the morning of June 27, was 1,500 to 1,800 warriors, but by the evening of the same day it had grown to 2,500; by July 4 to 3,000; and by 1879 to 8,000 to 9,000. Gray's calculations: about 1,000 lodges, slightly more than 7,000 people, possibly as many as 2,000 warriors if the older boys participated in the fighting.

Greasy Grass Ridge

North

Custer Battlefield Today

- ∘ *Marble marker*
- ● *Concentration of Army artifacts*
- ● *Concentration of Indian artifacts*
- ○ *Area of artifacts indicating positions*

CUSTER

BENTEEN

Reno Creek

CUSTER

WEIR

Reno Hill

Weir Point

RENO

North

Reno's Second Position

Reno's First Position

The Battlefield in 1876

- ⟵ *Known Army movement*
- ⟵--- *Inferred Army movement*
- ⟵ *Known Indian movement*
- ⟵--- *Inferred Indian movement*

1. *Northern Cheyenne Circle* 120 Lodges
2. *Hunkpapa Sioux Circle* 260 Lodges (including 25 lodges of Yanktonnais and Santee Sioux)
3. *Oglala Sioux Circle* 240 Lodges
4. *Miniconjou Sioux Circle* 150 Lodges
5. *Sans Arc Sioux Circle* 110 Lodges
6. *Combined Blackfoot, Brule, and Two Kettle Sioux Circle* 120 Lodges

Besides the Indians crossing the Little Bighorn at the Medicine Tail Ford, many crossed lower down the valley, at the mouth of a deep ravine draining the western slope of Battle Ridge. From this cover, they fired on Custer's flank on Calhoun Hill. To counter this threat, or perhaps even to find another ford by which to charge the village, Custer sent the troopers of Company C galloping down the side of the ridge to the head of the ravine. "The Indians hidden there got back quickly," said the Cheyenne woman Kate Big Head. The soldiers "stopped and got off their horses along another ridge, a low one just north of the deep gulch." They doubtless meant to fire into the ravine, but Lame White Man, a Cheyenne, hit them with a sudden attack that overran the company and scattered the survivors back to Calhoun Hill.

The final, desperate stage of the fighting occurred along Battle Ridge. While Keogh held Calhoun Hill against the warriors crossing at the mouth of Medicine Tail, Yates' two companies, probably accompanied by Custer, moved northward on the ridge. Custer may have been looking for a better defensive position or even, given his aggressive temperament, a way to get into the village. But the Indians converged in overpowering force from all directions. Fire from the east grew so hot that Yates' companies gathered for shelter on the western slope.

In the fighting with Custer's battalion, the Indians made few if any grand mounted charges. Mostly they kept up a long-range fire from dismounted positions behind hillocks, sagebrush clumps, tall grass, and in the folds and troughs of the terrain. From these places of concealment they struck down the cavalrymen with bullets from rifles, carbines, and pistols, some taken from Reno's dead in the valley, and old trade muskets. Arrows also took a heavy toll. Loosed in high arcs, they fell with deadly effect on clusters of exposed troopers.

The fatal blow fell from the north. As the fighting progressed from Medicine Tail Ford to Battle Ridge, Crazy Horse had led a large force of warriors down the Little Bighorn Valley to a crossing below the village, forded the river, and swept in a wide arc to climb Battle Ridge from the north. They struck the units with Custer and Yates and thrust up the ravine on the east leading to Calhoun Hill. Here they crushed Keogh's men against Gall's warriors beyond.

Gall, Hunkpapa war leader, led the frontal attack against Custer's column while Crazy Horse and Two Moon struck from flank and rear. His warriors had already routed Reno's men from the valley. Gall later claimed that at the time of the battle, the Sioux had no idea that they were fighting Custer; they thought they were fighting Crook.

French-born Lt. Edward G. Mathey of Company M commanded the pack train and took part in Reno's hilltop fight on June 25 and 26.

Although each of the companies made its "last stand," the last stand of history and legend occurred on the western slope of the northern end of Battle Ridge, now known as Custer Hill. Here Companies E and F and survivors of the other companies gathered around Custer's headquarters banner. Whether in panic or deliberate counterattack, a large contingent of soldiers broke toward the head of the deep ravine in the direction of the river. "We finished up this party right there in the ravine," said Red Horse. The rest, about 40, shot their horses for breastworks on the hillside and fought until all died. Among them were the three Custer brothers and nephew Autie Reed, Captain Yates, Adjutant Cooke, and Lts. Algernon E. Smith and William Van W. Reily. Keogh and Calhoun fell with their men to the south, and three officers were never found, or never identified.

The Sioux and Cheyennes, defending their homes and families, full of a sense of power and a conviction of injustice, did their work thoroughly. The soldiers fought back with a ferocity and bravery that earned high tribute from Sitting Bull himself. How long they fought before the last man fell is still debated—possibly two hours or more from Medicine Tail to Custer Hill.

Reno Besieged

Custer had plunged into battle without Captain Benteen's battalion, still a dozen miles back on the trail. Benteen's march to the left had taken him far enough to see into the Little Bighorn Valley and ensure that no Indians occupied that portion of it. He had then turned back on the trail of Custer and Reno, reaching it just in advance of Captain McDougall and the slow-moving pack train. A mile farther the battalion halted for 15 minutes at a swampy morass in the creek bed and watered their horses. The march continued through the old Sioux and Cheyenne campsite with its lone tipi, still burning. In another mile Sergeant Kanipe galloped up to Benteen, repeated Custer's orders, and continued back on the trail to find McDougall. Within the next mile Trumpeter Martin, his horse bleeding from a bullet wound in the hip, arrived with the penciled note from Cooke to bring the packs and be quick.

The note prompted Benteen to order a trot. Down Reno Creek the battalion pushed, approaching the

Little Bighorn in time to see the last of Reno's men retreating from the valley. One of the Crow scouts appeared and directed Benteen to the bluffs on his right, where the Reno survivors were gathering. A short gallop brought Benteen's companies to the heights. A few Indians pressed the position, but skirmishers quickly drove them back. Reno, hatless, a red bandana tied around his head, exclaimed: "For God's sake, Benteen, halt your command and help me. I've lost half my men."

Where was Custer, Benteen asked. Everyone else was asking the same question, but no one knew. The sound of heavy and continuous firing drifted down from the north, and two distinct volleys echoed over the hills. Neither Reno nor Benteen made any move to rush to the sound of the firing as required by the orders Martin had brought. Capt. Thomas B. Weir believed the distant firing should be investigated, and started toward Reno to urge it, then decided to ride along the bluffs to the north to see if he could learn more. His lieutenant, Winfield S. Edgerly, supposing that authority to move out had been granted, followed Weir with Company D. Later the remaining companies, reflecting the indecision of their leaders, strung out on Weir's trail, Company B and the pack train bringing up the rear.

Topping the high pinnacle now known as Weir Point, Weir scanned the terrain to the north. To the left lay the valley, full of tipis. To the front Weir Point fell away to Medicine Tail Coulee. Beyond, the land rose to distant hills and ridges obscured by rolling dust. Indistinctly amid the dust, recalled Lieutenant Edgerly, "We saw a good many Indians galloping up and down and firing at objects on the ground." Then, as Lt. Edward S. Godfrey recounted, "clouds of dust arose from all parts of the field, and the horsemen converged toward our position."

The warriors came up the north face of Weir Point, exhilarated by their triumph over Custer. The companies had deployed around the hill, but the battle had scarcely opened before they began to fall back. Reno himself, concerned for the wounded and the lagging pack train, had not come forward, and the withdrawal took place with the same lack of direction as the advance. Godfrey, commander of Company K, saw the danger of a disorderly retreat and, posting his men in a dismounted skirmish line,

*Dr. Henry R. Porter, shown here long after the fight, was the only one of three doctors attached to the 7th Cavalry during the 1876 campaign to survive the battle. The chief medical officer, Dr. George E. Lord (**below**), died with Custer, while Dr. James M. DeWolfe (**right**) was killed during Reno's flight from the valley. The site of Porter's field hospital, which he set up in a depression atop the bluffs during Reno's hilltop fight, can still be seen at the Reno-Benteen battlefield.*

held the Indians back while the rest of the command regained the original position on the bluff top.

The Indians pressed so closely that the troops had no chance to prepare a defense. Hastily dismounting, everyone hit the ground and, as Godfrey declared, "spread himself out as thin as possible." Carbine fire halted the Indian advance and drove the warriors to cover before they could overrun the position. The cavalry horses and pack mules were herded into a swale that offered a little shelter. Dr. Henry R. Porter, a civilian under contract to the Army and the only surviving doctor, had the wounded laid out in this natural depression, with the horses and mules providing uncertain protection from flying bullets and arrows.

"They pounded at us all of what was left of the first day," said Benteen. For three hours, until night brought relief, the beleagured cavalrymen endured a continuous and destructive fire from all sides. The warriors worked into positions close to the hilltop, kept their adversaries pinned down, and killed or wounded 11 soldiers. A few defenders managed to get behind a saddle or pack, but most considered themselves fortunate to have even a sagebrush in front of them.

Darkness fell about nine o'clock, and the firing ceased. Most of the Indians returned to the village for a great war dance illuminated by leaping bonfires—and for mourning rituals in recognition of their own dead. From Reno Hill the soldiers could hear the drums and chants and see the fires splashing the night sky.

The cavalrymen made good use of the hours of darkness, scooping out shallow entrenchments with knives, tin cups, mess gear, and any other tool that could supplement the handful of shovels with the pack train. From packs, ammunition boxes, saddles, and dead horses and mules they threw together makeshift barricades.

Some 350 soldiers and packers formed a circle around the depression where Porter had established his hospital. The swale resembled a saucer with the eastern side missing. Major Reno held the north rim of the saucer with most of the companies. Benteen occupied the south side, an elliptical ridge, with H Company. McDougall and Company B and Capt. Thomas H. French with Company M defended the west rim, from which the bluffs dropped precipitously to the Little Bighorn. Capt. Myles Moylan and Company A plugged the gap in the saucer on the east.

At first light, Trumpeter Martin sounded reveille, and a single rifle shot answered to open the second day of the Battle of the Little Bighorn. From all sides the Indians poured arrows and bullets into the defenses of Reno Hill. The soldiers, now dug in and better protected, fired back whenever a target offered, although the warriors proved adept at drawing fire without getting hit.

Throughout the hot morning the fight continued without letup. The Indians drew closer around the lines, taking skillful advantage of the irregular terrain and scattered sagebrush to stay hidden. At times they threatened to mass for an attack, especially on Benteen's exposed and thinly held position. Benteen himself strode about in full view, refusing to take cover and disdaining the fire directed at him. On one occasion he roused his men to their feet and led them in a charge that broke up a force of warriors gathering for an assault. On another he went to Reno and demanded a general counterattack. Led by Reno, the troopers rose from their pits and surged forward on all fronts to drive back the encircling Indians.

Thirst tormented the defenders, especially the wounded in the hospital area. Dr. Porter served notice that his charges must have water at any hazard. Four sharpshooters stood to distract the enemy and provide covering fire. A volunteer party slipped down a ravine to the river, filled canteens and camp kettles, and hastened back to the hilltop. They got little water, but it was enough to afford some relief to the wounded.

Early in the afternoon the fire began to slacken. By late afternoon only an occasional shot reminded the men to stay behind cover. In the valley, the Indians fired the dry prairie grass. A wall of thick smoke screened the village. About 7 p.m. an immense procession of horsemen, women and children on foot, travois, ponies, and dogs emerged from behind the smoke. Slowly it wound up the slope on the west side of the valley and made its way across the benchland to the southwest, toward the Big Horn Mountains. Below, the valley appeared deserted save for scattered debris of the great Indian camp.

Rescue

On Reno Hill the cavalrymen watched the exodus from the valley and speculated on its meaning. None knew what had happened to Custer. None knew why the Indians were leaving. None could shake the fear that the next morning would bring fresh waves of warriors against the hilltop. During the night the troops buried their dead and moved closer to the river. Lieutenant DeRudio and most of the soldiers and scouts left in the timber the day before made their way into the lines. They had remained concealed for a harrowing 36 hours while Indians came and went nearby.

Next morning a blue column could be seen approaching up the valley. Some thought it was Custer at last, others thought it was Terry. A few even guessed Crook. Two officers rode out to investigate. A short gallop brought them to the leading ranks of the 2d Cavalry, General Terry in the van. Both of Reno's officers burst out with the same question: Where is Custer?

Gibbon's chief of scouts, Lieutenant Bradley, had already discovered the answer. On Battle Ridge, four miles downstream, he had counted 197 corpses littering the ground. Of the five companies that followed Custer, apparently not a single man had survived, although the failure to account for all the bodies left a faint possibility that someone got away. Hundreds have since claimed to be the "only survivor" of the battle.

Altogether, half the 7th Cavalry lay dead or wounded. The troopers slain with Custer numbered 210. In Reno's retreat from the valley and his defense of the bluffs, another 53 were killed and 60 wounded. How many Indians paid for this victory with their lives will never be known, for most of the dead were borne off by the living. Estimates vary from 30 to 300. Indian accounts that tell of many wounded who died later suggest a figure closer to the latter than the former.

On the morning of June 28, Reno's men rode to the Custer battlefield to bury the dead. "A scene of sickening ghastly horror," Lieutenant Godfrey recalled. In accordance with Indian custom, most of the bodies had been stripped of their clothing and scalped and mutilated. They lay scattered about the battlefield where they had fallen. The bodies of

Custer and several of his officers lay with about 40 others on the western slope of Custer Hill. Although Cooke and Tom Custer had been badly butchered, most in this group escaped severe mutilation. "The bodies were as recognizable as if they were in life," Benteen wrote to his wife. Custer had been stripped but neither scalped nor mutilated. One bullet had hit his left breast, another his left temple. "His position was natural," observed Godfrey, "and one that we had seen hundreds of times while [he was] taking cat naps during halts on the march."

The dead were hastily buried. Tools were few, and in most cases the burial details simply scooped out a shallow grave and covered the body with a thin layer of sandy soil and some clumps of sagebrush. The officers were buried more securely and the graves plainly marked for future identification.

Not all was death on the battlefield. A few badly wounded cavalry horses were found, then destroyed. One was not. Comanche, Captain Keogh's claybank gelding, was spared and his wounds dressed. Never again put to work, Comanche survived for another 15 years, the 7th Cavalry's prized living trophy, venerated as the only true survivor of Custer's Last Battle.

Meanwhile, Reno's 60 wounded men required attention. Captain Marsh had succeeded in pushing the *Far West* up the Bighorn to the mouth of the Little Bighorn, and the crew laid beds of freshly cut grass on the deck to receive the wounded. Gibbon's troops improvised hand litters to carry them the 15 miles to the steamer. These proved too awkward and were replaced with litters rigged on poles strapped to two mules. On the morning of June 30 the wounded were carried aboard the *Far West*.

Cautiously, Captain Marsh piloted the *Far West* down the shallow Bighorn to its mouth. Here he waited for two days for Terry and Gibbon, then ferried their commands to the north side of the Yellowstone. On July 3 Marsh eased his craft into the muddy current for an epic voyage down the Yellowstone and the Missouri that became legendary in the history of river steamboating. At 11 p.m. on July 5, draped in black mourning cloth and flying the colors at half-mast, the *Far West* nosed into the Bismarck landing. Marsh had set a speed record never to be topped on the Missouri—710 miles in 54 hours.

While the crew ran around the sleeping town spreading the electrifying news, Marsh hastened to the telegraph office. The operator, J. M. Carnahan, seated himself at the key and tapped out a terse message: "Bismarck, D.T., July 5, 1876:—General Custer attacked the Indians June 25, and he, with every officer and man in five companies, were killed." It was the first of a series of dispatches that by the end of the next day totaled 50,000 words.

Meanwhile, the *Far West* dropped down the river to Fort Lincoln. The wounded were carried ashore and placed in the post hospital. In the predawn gloom of July 6, officers went from house to house waking the occupants and breaking the tragic news to the widows and orphans of the men who had fallen on the Little Bighorn.

Pursuit

Even as their comrades sought to overwhelm Major Reno's command on June 26, scouts from the village on the Little Bighorn brought word of more soldiers coming up the valley from the north. Rather than face this new threat, the Indians packed up and, as Reno's troopers watched from the bluff tops, pulled out of the valley to the southwest. So hastily did they decamp that they left some lodges standing and many of their possessions scattered about the site. But they departed exultantly, with soaring spirits, for never had they won a triumph so stunning and complete. For several nights their camps rang with victory celebrations.

Already as they withdrew before Terry's advance the great village had grown too unwieldy. Game had taken flight, and hunters could not find enough meat to feed so many people. Within two days, small groups began to spin off, to go their own way or head back to the agencies. Nearing Crook's base on Goose Creek, war parties from these groups mauled a scouting detachment from his command and even tried to burn him out of his camp by firing the prairie grass. The main village of Indians crossed from the upper Little Bighorn back to the Rosebud, dropped down that stream a short distance, then turned east to the Tongue. They traveled rapidly, searching for buffalo. To discourage pursuit, they set huge grass fires behind them.

Both Crook and Terry lay paralyzed in their base

Chartered by the Government for the campaign of 1876, the Far West *performed important service in transporting troops, supplies, and dispatches. With Reno's wounded on board, the boat steamed from the mouth of the Bighorn to Bismarck, 710 miles, in 54 hours—a record unsurpassed in steamboating on the Upper Missouri.*

camps, Crook near the head of Tongue River, Terry on the Yellowstone at the mouth of the Bighorn. The enormity of the Custer disaster, news of which finally reached Crook on July 10, traumatized both generals and all their subordinates. Almost at once they began to imagine themselves opposed by many times the actual number of warriors who had inflicted the defeat on Custer, and they feared a like fate if they ventured forth without heavy reinforcement.

More troops were on the way. The news of the Little Bighorn had shocked and outraged the American people, and newspapers cried for swift reprisal. Sheridan had fresh troops under orders as soon as he received Terry's first dispatches from the Yellowstone. Although Sheridan impatiently urged Crook "to hit them again and hit them hard," neither general would move without the additional units.

It was the first week in August by the time the reinforcements arrived and the two forces got underway. By then the fugitive Indians had scattered even more, with the main camp now still farther to the east, in the lower Powder Valley. Some of the agency groups had already reached the western edge of the Great Sioux Reservation, and a few had even reported themselves at the agencies. On August 7, Terry, who had moved down the Yellowstone to the mouth of the Rosebud, started up that stream on Custer's old trail with about 1,700 infantry and cavalry. Crook had started down the Tongue three days earlier with close to 2,300 men, but had soon turned west to the Rosebud, where he picked up the Indian trail. On August 10, to the surprise of all, the two columns met.

At this point the Indian trail, now more than a month old, veered eastward toward the Tongue. Joining forces, the two generals led their army of 4,000 in pursuit. Night after night cold rain drenched the lightly clad soldiers, and day after day they slogged through the mud trying to catch up with the Indians. Horses weakened, the shoes of the infantry shredded, morale sank, and sickness and fatigue afflicted the exhausted ranks.

Weary and dispirited, the army reached the Yellowstone at the mouth of the Powder on August 17. It had labored in vain. Never had it come closer than a hundred miles to any sizable body of Indians. At least a week earlier, in fact, still farther to the east,

Custer battlefield looking southwest about 3 years after the fight. Wooden stakes mark the graves of the dead on Custer Hill. Each stake contained an empty shell casing holding the name of the grave's occupant, if it was known. The Little Bighorn River lies beyond the tree line in the distance. Beyond that is the valley in which the large Indian village was located.

Captain Keogh's marker. In the summer of 1877, Captain Keogh's reconstituted Company I returned to the battlefield to reclaim the bodies of the officers and rebury those of the enlisted men. Two years later the graves were remounded by a burial party under Capt. George K. Sanderson of the 11th Infantry, shown here looking at Keogh's marker on the spot where he fell.

Captain Keogh's claybank gelding, Comanche, was near death from arrow and bullet wounds when it was found on the battlefield. The horse was taken to Fort Lincoln and nursed back to health. It lived another 15 years, dying in 1891 at the age of 28. Holding the reins is blacksmith Gustave Korn, a former private in Keogh's Company I who served as the horse's keeper until his death at the Battle of Wounded Knee in 1890.

the remaining core of the Indian village had fragmented and scattered. Sitting Bull took his people northeast to the lower Little Missouri. Crazy Horse and the Oglalas turned south toward the Black Hills.

As the rains continued, Terry and Crook floundered in mud and indecision while also trying to stockpile enough provisions to resume the chase. Steamboats pushed up from Bismarck with supplies, fighting for time as the river fell. The two generals bickered over what to do next. Terry, fearful that Sitting Bull and other Hunkpapas would break to the north, wanted Crook to cooperate in operations to the northeast, along the lower Yellowstone. Crook, on the other hand, fretted over Indians heading south, toward the Red Cloud and Spotted Tail agencies; these lay in the Department of the Platte, now uncovered by his absence in Terry's department, and he wanted to get back to his own area of responsibility.

At length, at the beginning of September, they went their separate ways. Terry made some hesitant probes in several directions, then abandoned the field, sending most of his army back to their stations. Crook pointed directly east, on the Terry-Custer trail of the previous spring, looking for Indian sign.

Crook cut loose from Terry and the river supply line with but scanty provisions, and within two days the men were on half rations. The bad weather continued, adding rain, fog, and heavy mud to the growing hunger. "Wet, cross, hungry, disgusted," noted the general's aide in his diary, reflecting not only fatigue, discomfort, and short rations but also puzzlement over their leader's intentions, which he shared with no one. Finally, east of the Little Missouri, he decided on a quick dash to the Black Hills, 175 miles away.

What followed is known to history as "Crook's Starvation March." For nearly a week the column struggled through constant rain, fog, and heavy mud in a nightmarish ordeal that pushed exhausted men to the edge of collapse and dropped animals by the score. Rations gave out, and stringy meat cut from butchered horses and mules afforded the only fare. Faced with calamity, Crook on September 8 dispatched a mule train to push ahead to Deadwood and buy food on the open market. Capt. Anson Mills and 150 cavalrymen mounted on the strongest remaining animals went along as escort.

Preoccupied with more immediate problems, no one thought much about Indians. But near Slim Buttes, Mills turned up 37 Oglala lodges and at dawn on September 9 charged into the sleeping camp. Crook came up in the afternoon, and the troops wiped out the last pockets of resistance. American Horse, the chief, died from wounds received in the fight, and the lodges were all destroyed. From the Indian stores the starving soldiers at last obtained food.

American Horse's band proved but an outlier of a camp of nearly a hundred lodges under Crazy Horse. Some 200 warriors rode to the attack and fell on Crook's 2,000. In the evening and next morning the Oglalas stabbed at defensive lines posted by Crook, then drew off as the army resumed its march toward the Black Hills. The weary, ragged, miserable soldiers, and their officers as well, had lost all incentive for a decisive fight with the Sioux.

Not until September 13 did the terrible trek draw to a close. On that day a herd of beef cattle and a train of wagons loaded with provisions met the column and ended the "Starvation March." Thus ended, too, the summer campaign of 1876. For all the effort, it could boast but one success—the modest and accidental victory at Slim Buttes.

War's End

The annihilation of Custer's command brought the wrath of the nation down upon the Sioux and Cheyennes at the agencies as well as those out in the Powder and Yellowstone country. General Sheridan, authorized to impose military rule, began by dismounting and disarming the Indians at the agencies, many of whom had not been absent during the summer. Also, backed by a stern congressional mandate, a commission visited the agencies in September 1876 to demand the sale of the Black Hills. The chiefs had no choice but to "touch the pen," thus giving legal validity to a transaction aggressive miners had already made an accomplished fact. Confronted with the harsh treatment at the agencies, many Indians who had come in to give up promptly turned about and rejoined their roaming brethren.

Nor did the Army abandon all effort to subjugate the roamers. Terry had left troops to hold the Yellowstone through the winter and, in the spring,

Would Gatling Guns Have Saved Custer?

Yes, argued Gen. Henry J. Hunt, who had commanded the Army of the Potomac's artillery in the Civil War, a Gatling battery "would probably have saved the command" and the day as well. Drawn by condemned cavalry horses and manned by infantrymen, the Gatling gun pictured here at Fort Lincoln was one of three that accompanied General Terry's column. Terry offered them to Custer on June 21, together with Maj. James Brisbin's battalion of the Second Cavalry. Custer refused. The Gatlings, he said, would slow his march. Emplaced atop Custer Hill, the three Gatlings might well have saved the day. By turning a crank and feeding ammunition into a hopper, a Gatling crew could spew up to 350 rounds a minute from the bank of revolving barrels. Such fire power might have held the Indians at bay until help came or even stampeded them.

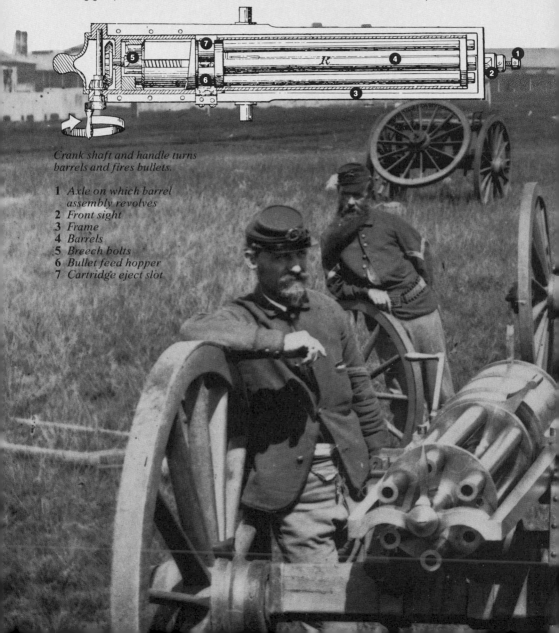

Crank shaft and handle turns barrels and fires bullets.

1 *Axle on which barrel assembly revolves*
2 *Front sight*
3 *Frame*
4 *Barrels*
5 *Breech bolts*
6 *Bullet feed hopper*
7 *Cartridge eject slot*

On the other hand, Gatlings were temperamental. They easily fouled by residue from black powder cartridges and often jammed when overheated. Also, as Custer observed, they were slow and cumbersome on the trail. As it turned out, Terry's battery had a hard time even keeping up with Gibbon's infantry. "They are worthless for Indian fighting," attested Gen. Nelson A. Miles.

Thus it is difficult to conceive of any circumstances in which the Gatling guns would still have been with Custer when he reached the hill where he died. Surely the restless, impatient Custer would not have let them hold back his swift march to the Little Bighorn. At best they would have been consigned to the pack train when he divided the regiment, at worst left somewhere back on the trail to catch up as speedily as possible.

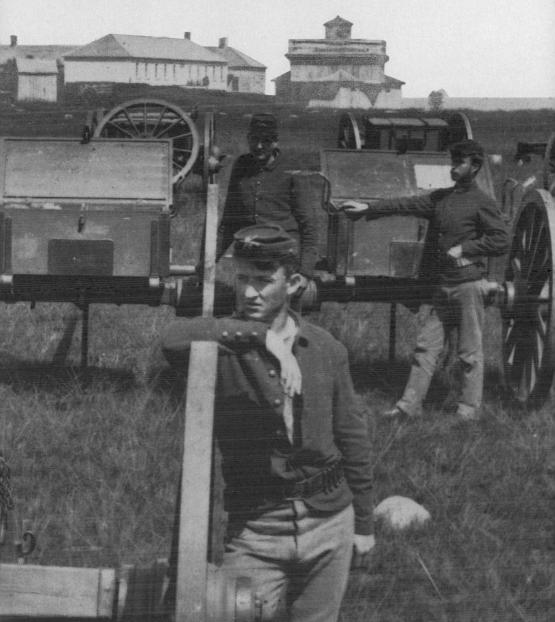

build two permanent forts that Sheridan had persuaded Congress were essential to the pacification of the northern Plains. They threw up a temporary cantonment at the mouth of the Tongue River, but they did not while away the winter in their huts. Their young and ambitious commander, Col. Nelson A. Miles, was a friend and admirer of Custer and a practitioner of his aggressive, hard-hitting style of war. Clothing his infantrymen in buffalo overcoats and other cold-weather gear, he campaigned all through the hard winter months. "Bear's Coat," the Indians named him.

Crook also fielded a winter expedition, this time with better results. Leading his striking arm was another of the Army's vigorous young colonels, Ranald S. Mackenzie. In the misty dawn of November 25, 1876, Mackenzie and 1,100 horsemen burst into the Cheyenne village of Dull Knife and Little Wolf, 183 lodges hidden in a canyon of the Red Fork of Powder River. The Cheyennes lost their tipis, stores of food and clothing, and pony herd. Crazy Horse took them in, but they no longer had the will to resist.

By the spring of 1877, Indians by the hundreds began to drift into the agencies and surrender. Even Crazy Horse saw the futility of holding out longer. On May 6, 1877, he led a procession of more than 1,100 Sioux into Camp Robinson, Nebraska, and threw his weapons on the ground. Less than six months later he was dead, killed in a guardhouse scuffle. "It is good," observed one of the agency chiefs; "he has looked for death, and it has come."

Sitting Bull chose another course. Vowing never to submit, he led some 400 Hunkpapas across the boundary into Canada. But food was scarce, and Miles' soldiers guarded the border to prevent the Indians from hunting buffalo in Montana. Little by little the refugees weakened. First Gall, then Crow King brought their followers to Fort Buford to surrender. At last, in July 1881, Sitting Bull and 43 families appeared at the fort. Facing the commanding officer, he declared: "I wish it to be remembered that I was the last man of my tribe to surrender my rifle, and this day have given it to you."

Sitting Bull's surrender formally marked the end of a war that had all but ended four years earlier, when most of the Indians who fought the soldiers in

1876 settled on the reservation. In their triumph at the Little Bighorn, the Sioux and Cheyennes had awakened forces that led to their collapse. The campaign of 1876 had, after all, accomplished the objectives set by its planners. It had forced the Indians to abandon the unceded territory and accept Government control on the reservation. And it had frightened the chiefs into selling the Black Hills.

The Sioux and Cheyennes bitterly submitted to the reservation way of life. Although it contrasted cruelly with the old ways, gradually they came to see that the freedom of the past could never be recaptured. For a generation to come, however, old warriors would recall with satisfaction the brief moment of glory when they wiped out Long Hair and his bluecoats.

Why?

How could it have happened? The question reverberated up and down the Army chain of command and quickly spilled over into the newspapers and public journals. It was the subject of a court of inquiry that raked over Major Reno's every act and decision without finding the answer (or charging Reno). And it has echoed through history to this day.

The simplest explanation, usually overlooked in the endless debates over strategy and tactics, is that the Army lost because the Indians won. They were strong, united, well led, well armed, confident, and outraged by the Government's war aims. Rarely had the Army encountered such a powerful combination in an Indian adversary.

But this explanation exonerates all the military chiefs and permits no scapegoat in blue. The search for one began at once and has been diligently pursued for more than a century. In turn, Terry, Gibbon, Crook, Custer, Reno, and Benteen have been indicted. And not capriciously. For if the blame must fall entirely on the Army, all bear more or less responsibility.

The largest current of thought washes up Custer as the culprit. Thirsting for glory, he was accused of disobeying Terry's orders, taking a direct instead of circuitous route to his destination, attacking with an exhausted command and without adequate reconnaissance, and at the last moment dividing his force in the face of a superior adversary. All these charges

The Reno Court of Inquiry

Inevitably, the search for someone to blame focused on Custer's second-in-command, Maj. Marcus A. Reno. Custer's first biographer, Frederick Whittaker, charged Reno with cowardice in failing to rush to his commander's aid. Whittaker's thick volume, rushed into print within six months of the battle, demanded that the Army launch an investigation. Reno himself requested an official inquiry.

The Reno Court of Inquiry convened at Chicago's Palmer House on January 13, 1879. Trim in colorful dress uniforms, the witnesses and officers of the court attracted wide attention, both in Chicago and throughout the nation. The judges, two colonels and a lieutenant colonel, sat for four weeks and heard the testimony of 23 witnesses. Most of the surviving officers who had fought at the Little Bighorn, a

few enlisted men, civilian participants, and Major Reno himself (shown seated in front of the right window in this newspaper woodcut of the trial) took the stand to give their version of what happened and why.

Although conducted under military law and procedure, a court of inquiry can only recommend further judicial proceedings. The task of the Reno Court of Inquiry was not to assess guilt but to determine

whether enough evidence existed to warrant trying Major Reno before a court-martial.

Ably defended by civilian counsel, and perhaps aided by officers reluctant to bring disgrace on the 7th Cavalry, Reno emerged from the ordeal with the court's halfhearted vindication. The finding: "While subordinates in some instances, did more for the safety of the command by brilliant displays of courage than did Major Reno, there was nothing in his conduct which requires animadversion from this Court."

The court's conclusion hardly stilled the debate; in fact it only stoked new disputes. Reno did not participate. Court-martialed on other, unrelated charges, he was dismissed from the Army and died a decade later, a broken man. The controversies lived on, however, and whether Reno could have saved Custer, or should have tried, is vehemently argued to this day.

For historians, the record of the Reno Court of Inquiry is invaluable. Ironically, though, this mountain of first-hand evidence has brought students no closer to definitive answers than it did the judges who first pondered it more than a century ago.

The Faces on the Bar Room Wall

No faces in American history have inspired greater boozy contemplation than those of the Adams-Becker rendering (below) of the men who struggled atop Custer Hill on June 25, 1876. Cassilly Adams painted the original in 1886—a huge, stilted, undramatic composition intended as a travel-ing exhibition. But it remained for Otto Becker, recreating the canvas in 1896 for a lithograph by the Anheuser-Busch Brewing Company, to beget the version (shown here) that adorned the saloon walls of the nation for a generation. Ultimately, a million copies of the Becker print rolled off the presses, prompting one authority to speculate that it had been viewed by more lowbrows and fewer art critics than any other picture in American history.

The Adams-Becker painting is by all odds the best known, but hardly the only one, and assuredly not the most fanci-ful. In the late 1960s the staff

of the Amon Carter Museum in Fort Worth attempted to catalogue the many pictures of the Custer fight. Each of the more than 900 versions identified is, of course, the product of the artist's imagination. In a situation where imagination may properly replace truth (no witness survived to contest the artist), it is curious that almost every artist to the present time has been absorbed in the reality of the event and has neglected the human overtones: the sullen quiet of the Indian betrayed, the sudden surprise and totality of death on the vast plains, the frustration of hindsight judgments, the responsibilities and loyalties obliterated in the aftermath. There were no victors that day, just survivors, each aware that a day of reckoning had passed and another would soon be upon them. As in any disaster, many people learned much, but too late.

can be refuted or plausibly explained; yet as every officer knows, the commander bears ultimate responsibility for the success or failure of his command, and George Armstrong Custer cannot escape this basic military maxim.

A truer explanation is simply that Custer's legendary luck deserted him. Circumstance piled on circumstance to make him their victim. Circumstance—bad luck—appeared to reveal him to his enemy prematurely and forced him into battle before he intended. Knowing neither terrain nor the exact location or strength of the Indian camp, he had to grope forward half blindly, allowing his battle plan to take shape as circumstances unfolded. By the time he knew enough for informed action, it was too late. Benteen had been sent beyond timely recall, and Reno had been committed to battle—both defensible actions when taken. It remained only to throw his own immediate command against the Indians, and even that effort faltered on enemy opposition and difficult terrain. The altered timetable, moreover, precipitated battle in the afternoon rather than at dawn, the preferred time, when Indians tended to be least alert.

Reno ranks next as favored scapegoat. Critics score him for not pushing his charge against the Indian camp or at least for not holding his position in the timber. Reno's retreat freed large numbers of Indians to concentrate on Custer at a crucial stage of the action. Had Reno continued to fight in the valley, the pressure on Custer might well have been decisively lessened. What cannot be known is whether such a course would have rewarded Reno with the same fate as Custer. Significantly, those who followed Reno into the valley condemned not the decision to withdraw, only the execution.

More vulnerable is Reno's management of the hilltop operation. A strong case can be made that he should have rushed to Custer's aid no matter what the odds and even at the risk of disaster. The written orders to Benteen, now Reno's by virtue of superior rank, explicitly required such a move. In addition, some of his officers urged this course on him. In fact, Reno made no decision, and his indecision freed subordinates to go off on their own and in the end endangered the entire command. Thereafter, through a night and day of defensive action, Reno failed to exert effective command. Indeed, there is strong evidence that he proposed to pull out altogether, abandoning the wounded, a proposition that Benteen indignantly rejected. Otherwise, Reno did not behave discreditably, but no one doubted that Benteen functioned as the true commander.

For his part, Captain Benteen failed his superior at a critical point. Disgruntled over his "valley hunting" assignment, he lingered on the backtrail. With battle unmistakably joined, even two urgent messages from Custer could not speed his pace. Both left no doubt that Custer wanted him and the ammunition packs just as swiftly as Benteen could get them there. Instead he kept to the trail, joined Reno, and let him determine what moves, if any, would next be attempted. In the fight for the bluffs, on the other hand, Benteen's strong leadership and cool bravery contributed greatly to the successful defense.

Others invite criticism. Neither before nor after the Little Bighorn did Terry, Gibbon, or Crook gather and use intelligence in a thoughtful way. Gibbon repeatedly let opportunity slip from his grasp and failed to keep Terry fully informed. Crook mismanaged both his March and June offensives, withdrawing on both occasions with questionable justification. The latter, after the Rosebud, left Custer to confront the entire Indian strength alone. Privately, General Sherman believed that Crook bore large responsibility for the failure of the campaign of 1876.

And yet, in dissecting strategy and tactics from the perspective of a century later, it is easy to do injustice to the responsible commanders. One cannot know fully all the circumstances of the enemy, weather, terrain, troops, weapons, and a host of other factors great and trivial that influenced judgment and sometimes decisively shaped the final outcome. In particular, an officer—or any historic person, for that matter—should be judged solely on the basis of what he knew or could reasonably foresee at a particular time, not on what we know now. In few events is this principle more pertinent than the Battle of the Little Bighorn.

To load so much blame on the military officers is to do disservice to the Indians. They fought well that day. Perhaps no strategy or tactics could have prevailed against Sitting Bull's powerful medicine.

Part 3

Little Bighorn Battlefield Today

From Battlefield to National Monument

Almost overnight the site of the Battle of the Little Bighorn became a national shrine and tourist attraction. Its care fell to the Army, which in 1877 built Fort Custer 15 miles to the north. A year after the battle, Captain Keogh's old Company I of the 7th Cavalry, now reconstituted, returned to comb the battlefield and exhume the bodies of Custer and 11 other officers and two civilians for reinterment elsewhere. In accordance with Custer's wishes, his widow had his remains reburied at the United States Military Academy at West Point, N.Y.

In 1879 the battlefield was designated a national cemetery, and the Fort Custer troopers worked to make it more presentable. On top of Custer Hill they erected a log memorial. They remounded the scattered graves and marked each with a substantial wooden stake. In 1881 an imposing granite monument, bearing the names of all the slain, arrived at the Fort Custer landing and soon replaced the log memorial on Custer Hill. At the same time, the remains of the fallen troopers were exhumed from their individual graves and reinterred in a common grave around the base of the monument. In 1890 white marble headstones replaced the wooden stakes marking the original graves and thus formed a rough guide to where the soldiers had been killed.

As Indian warfare subsided, the Army began to abandon its frontier forts. Custer Battlefield National Cemetery offered a convenient place to move the bodies buried in the various post cemeteries. Gradually the dead from other Indian battles took their place in the national cemetery at the foot of Custer Hill. They serve as reminders of the whole sweep of military history on the northern Great Plains.

The first battlefield superintendent arrived in 1893. For almost 50 years afterward, a succession of War Department officials cared for the area. Many were retired soldiers, some veterans of the Sioux campaign of 1876. Their personal knowledge of the battle served them well in dealing with the growing number of visitors. People came, the custodians discovered, not so much to visit the national cemetery as to see the scene of "Custer's Last Stand." Many were avid relic hunters and curiosity seekers and often carried off mementos ranging from cartridge cases to human bones and, above all, fragments of the marble headstones.

In 1940 stewardship passed from the War Department to the National Park Service of the Department of the Interior. Reflecting the changed emphasis on historic site rather than active cemetery, in 1946 Custer Battlefield National Cemetery was renamed Custer Battlefield National Monument. Preserving and interpreting the battlefield now became the principal mission.

Interpretation underwent changes, too. Originally established to pay homage to the fallen soldiers and white civilians, the battlefield came gradually to stand for the Indian side of the story as well, and interpretation expanded to fill the void. This new emphasis is reflected in the 1992 legislation that resulted once again in changing the name of the park, this time to Little Bighorn Battlefield National Monument. Today the battlefield fittingly commemorates not only the westward advance of the American frontier but also the last phases of the Indians' struggle to retain their lands and way of life. Modern Indians, some descendants of those who fought Custer and others of Indian scouts who served Custer, share with white interpreters the task of explaining the Battle of the Little Bighorn to the hundreds of thousands of visitors who come to the battlefield each year.

The following guide highlights the principal battlefield features.

Custer Hill, looking north from Weir Point.

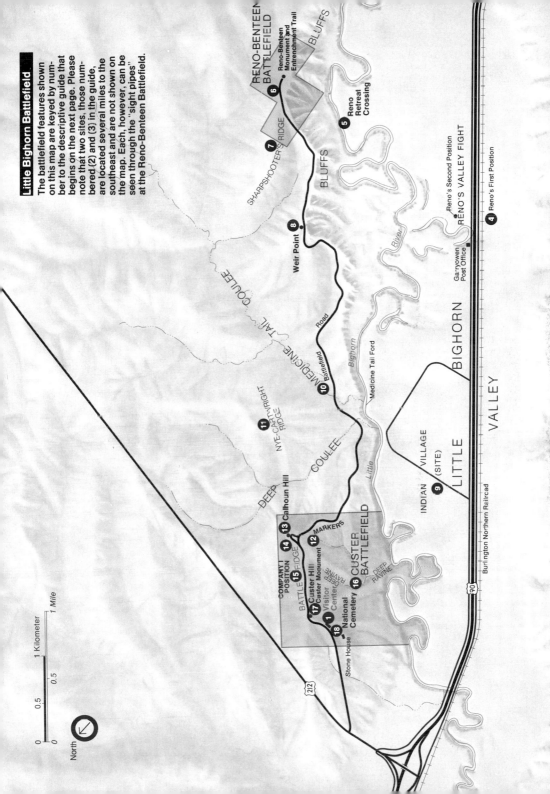

Little Bighorn Battlefield

The battlefield features shown on this map are keyed by number to the descriptive guide that begins on the next page. Please note that two sites, those numbered (2) and (3) in the guide, are located several miles to the southeast and are not shown on the map. Each, however, can be seen through the "sight pipes" at the Reno-Benteen Battlefield.

North

0   0.5   1 Kilometer
0   0.5   1 Mile

RENO-BENTEEN BATTLEFIELD

BLUFFS

6 Reno-Benteen Monument and Entrenchment Trail

5 Reno Retreat Crossing

7 SHARPSHOOTER'S RIDGE

BLUFFS

BLUFFS

Reno's Second Position

RENO'S VALLEY FIGHT

4 Reno's First Position

8 Weir Point

MEDICINE TAIL COULEE

Ga'ryowen Post Office

River

Battlefield Road

Bighorn

Medicine Tail Ford

10

NYE-CARTWRIGHT RIDGE

11

DEEP COULEE

Little

LITTLE

BIGHORN

VALLEY

INDIAN VILLAGE (SITE)

9

Calhoun Hill

13

COMPANY I POSITION

14

MARKERS

12

15 Custer Hill

BATTLE RIDGE

DEEP RAVINE

16 CUSTER BATTLEFIELD

DEEP RAVINE

17 Custer Monument

1 Visitor Center

18 National Cemetery

Stone House

212

Burlington Northern Railroad

90

❶ Visitor Center

The exhibits and interpretive programs here will help you understand the battle, and the ground on which it was fought. The museum features numerous military and Indian artifacts, artwork, dioramas, and audiovisual programs dealing with the Sioux War of 1876, the battle, and the lives of soldiers and Indians. The visitor center is also depository for significant collections of documents and memorabilia, including the Elizabeth B. Custer Collection of more than 5,000 letters and other papers.

The battle is best understood by beginning the battlefield tour at the Reno-Benteen Battlefield 4.5 miles from the visitor center. Wayside exhibits will then be in sequence on the return trip. This guide is arranged in the same order. Consult the map on page 95 for orientation.

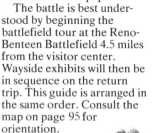

*Among the park's Indian artifacts are (**above and left**) a pair of beaded moccasins that purportedly belonged to Sitting Bull, and a Sioux war bonnet.* **Opposite**: *The park's 7th Cavalry collection includes the uniform coat of Sgt. William Williams (a private in Company H at the time of the battle); a buckskin jacket owned by Lt. Col. George A. Custer; Lt. W. W. Cooke's dress helmet; one of Capt. Thomas Custer's regimental shoulder knots; and Lt. Colonel Custer's commission.*

Archeology on the Battlefield, 1984 and 1985

In August 1983 a prairie fire swept over Custer Battlefield consuming nearly 600 acres of the 640-acre site. With the battlefield stripped of vegetation, the National Park Service saw an opportunity to initiate an archeological investigation, hoping the barren hills and ravines would reveal some of the battle's closely guarded secrets. For five weeks in the spring of 1984 and again in 1985, a team of archeologists and volunteers combed the park. Nearly 5,000 artifacts were recovered, yielding primarily expended cartridges,

like those shown at right, fired by soldier or brave during the battle and aiding in site identification of Indian positions. Excavations around marble markers placed on the field in 1890 to show where soldiers had been originally interred (they were exhumed in 1881 and placed in a mass grave at the top of Custer Hill) produced a scattering of human bones missed in previous reburial efforts. More importantly, the excavations substantiated the historical record that the markers are reasonably accurate in approximating where

soldiers had been buried. But even with the abundance of new material, the archeological survey has not altered appreciably the interpretation of the battle. Custer's route over the battlefield, the positioning of the troops on the field, and the details on how his command was wiped out still remain part of the battlefield's enduring mysteries. Archeological excavations in 1984-85 failed to solve the riddle.

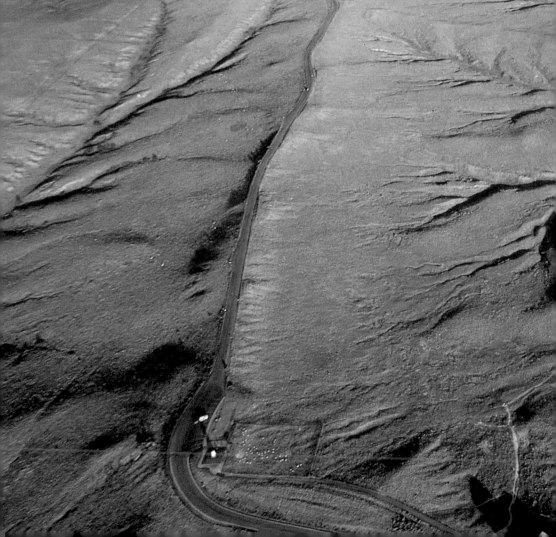

❷ Wolf Mountains and Crow's Nest

Standing at the monument on the Reno-Benteen Battlefield, face to the southeast, or your left. The mountains on the skyline are the Wolf Mountains, or "Chadeesh," as the Crow Indians called them. They divide the drainages of the Rosebud and Little Bighorn valleys. To your left, near a low saddle in the northern end of the mountains, is a promontory the Crows called the Crow's Nest. Before sunrise on June 25, 1876, Custer's Crow and Arikara scouts, ranging in advance of the 7th Cavalry, climbed this lookout. From here they sighted the Indian encampment in the Little Bighorn Valley 15 miles distant.

❸ Reno Creek and Lone Tipi Site

Custer's approach to the Little Bighorn lay down the narrow valley of a stream then known as Sundance or Ash Creek but later named Reno Creek in honor of Major Reno. The creek rises in the low pass through the northern end of the Wolf Mountains mentioned above. A thread of timber marking the lower part is visible from the Reno-Benteen Battlefield. Along this stretch of the stream, at a site never conclusively identified, stood the "lone tipi." Left standing when the Sioux moved a week earlier, this tipi contained the body of a warrior killed at the Battle of the Rosebud. At this point scouts reported enemy warriors to the front, and Custer ordered Major Reno in pursuit.

❹ Reno's Valley Fight

Looking west and slightly to the right from the Reno-

Reno Creek, looking northeast.

Site of Reno's retreat across the Little Bighorn River.

Custer's view of Reno's valley fight from the bluffs.

Benteen monument, one sees the Garryowen Post Office at a point on the highway and railroad where a timbered bend of the Little Bighorn River sweeps almost across the valley. Immediately to the right, or north, of this point lay the upper end of the Sioux and Cheyenne Indian village. After crossing the river at the mouth of Reno Creek, Reno and his command advanced down the valley this far. Opposed here by several hundred mounted warriors, he dismounted his troopers in a thin skirmish line. Quickly outflanked, he withdrew them to the timber on his right. This, too, proved untenable, and he led his men in retreat across the open valley in the foreground toward the bluffs where the monument is located.

❺ Reno Retreat Crossing
Repeated assaults on both flanks and rear of Reno's retreating column made crossing the Little Bighorn River difficult and dangerous. Recalled Lt. Luther R. Hare: "The crossing was not covered and no effort was made to hold the Indians back. . . . If the Indians had followed us in force to the hill-top, they would have got us all."

101

6 Reno-Benteen Battlefield

After retreating from the valley to the bluffs, Reno and his shattered command took positions in the vicinity of the present Reno-Benteen monument. Here Reno was shortly joined by Captain Benteen and his battalion and, soon afterward, by Captain McDougall and the packtrain. After wiping out Custer four miles to the north, the Sioux and Cheyenne warriors laid siege to Reno at this site. The command, about 400 strong, entrenched in a rough circle around the saucer-like depression just south of the monument. In this sheltered swale, Dr. Porter established the hospital. Beginning at the monument, Entrenchment Trail provides an interpretive tour of Reno's defensive positions.

7 Sharpshooter's Ridge

From the Reno-Benteen parking area, proceed 0.4 mile back along the tour road. To your right, parallel to the road and 200 yards distant, is a long ridge that took its name from an unusually skilled Indian marksman. Recalled 1st Sgt. John Ryan: "There was a high ridge on the right and one Indian in particular I must give credit for being a good shot. While we were lying in the line he fired a shot and killed the fourth man on my right. Soon afterward he fired again and shot the third man. His third shot wounded the man on my right, who jumped back from the line and down among the rest of the wounded. I thought my turn was coming next. I jumped up with Captain French, and some half a dozen members of my company and, instead of firing straight to the front, as we had been doing, . . . we

Hospital site on Reno-Benteen Battlefield.

Site of the Indian village, from the base of Weir Point.

Sharpshooter's Ridge from Reno-Benteen Battlefield.

wheeled to our right and put in a deadly volley, and I think we put an end to that Indian, as there were no more men killed at that particular spot."

❽ Weir Point

A drive of 1.2 miles on the road back toward Custer Battlefield leads to a high peak through which the road has been cut. Named for Capt. Thomas B. Weir, this marks the limit of advance by elements of Major Reno's command in the effort to open communications with Custer. A brisk skirmish occurred here with hundreds of warriors returning from the Custer Battlefield, and Reno's men were ordered to withdraw to the blufftop positions where the monument now stands.

❾ Indian Village

Approaching Weir Point and descending its north face, the tour road affords good views of the Little Bighorn Valley to the west. This was the site of the Indian village. Custer first glimpsed it from the bluffs near where Reno and Benteen later fought. Approximately three miles long, the village covered much of the valley west of the river from present Garryowen Post Office to a point almost opposite Battle Ridge.

❿ Medicine Tail Coulee

From Weir Point the tour road drops 1.6 miles to the crossing of Medicine Tail Coulee. To the west about 300 yards the coulee empties into the Little Bighorn River. Descending Medicine Tail Coulee, part of Custer's command encountered Indians at its mouth and, after an exchange of fire and possibly some casualties, retreated to the north and east to Battle Ridge.

103

⑪ Nye-Cartwright Ridge

Named for two students of the battle who discovered firing positions marked by expended cartridge cases, Nye-Cartwright Ridge lies one-half mile east of the marker denoting where Sgt. James Butler was found. The ridge forms part of the divide between Medicine Tail and Deep Coulees. A battalion of Custer's force fought dismounted defensive actions on this ridge before moving on to Battle Ridge. How the troopers got here is one of the battle's imponderables. Some believe they may have become separated from the rest of the command as a result of Indian gunfire in Medicine Tail Coulee. Others think that the men were deployed to keep warriors from enveloping Custer's right flank. Still others maintain that the soldiers were posted on the ridge to protect the expected approach of the packtrain as it emerged into Medicine Tail Coulee.

⑫ Markers

From Medicine Tail Coulee the tour road rises 1.1 miles to the south entrance to the Custer Battlefield. From here to the monument at the north end of Battle Ridge, the road affords a view of the terrain over which Custer's command fought with Sioux and Cheyenne warriors in the final death struggle. White marble markers may be seen in seemingly random pattern on both sides of the road. Although some are known to be misplaced, most of them mark the locations where the bodies of slain troopers were buried immediately after the battle. Since the dead soldiers were buried at or very near where they fell, these markers sketch in rough outline

Nye-Cartwright Ridge.

Where Lt. James Calhoun fell.

104

Calhoun Hill, looking southeast from Custer Hill.

Captain Keogh's I Company position.

the progress of the fighting. All the remains were later reinterred in a common grave at the monument, so these markers do not now identify graves. No markers show where Indians fell. The bodies of dead warriors were removed from the field and later placed in tipis or caves.

⓭ Calhoun Hill
From the south entrance the route lies between markers on both sides of the roadway. (The markers probably indicate where men of Company C fell.) The road continues to a loop around the perimeter of Calhoun Hill. Here the two parts of Custer's command that had fought at the mouth of Medicine Tail and on Nye-Cartwright Ridge probably reunited and began the movement along the top of Battle Ridge to the north. In the final actions, Lt. James Calhoun's Company L fought and died at this position.

⓮ Battle Ridge
The tour road follows the crest of Battle Ridge between Calhoun Hill and the monument on Custer Hill. Fighting northward along this ridge, Custer's command came finally to its last stand near the present monument.

⓯ Company I Position
The markers scattered along the east slope of Battle Ridge between Calhoun Hill and Custer Hill represent the destruction of Capt. Myles W. Keogh's Company I. Keogh's body was found amid a cluster of his own men and a few from Company C. A charge up this drainage from the north led by Crazy Horse is usually credited with destroying Keogh's command.

Next page: *Custer Hill*

16 Deep Ravine

West of Battle Ridge, toward the river, Deep Ravine was the scene of heavy fighting. No headstones today represent this action, but ample evidence testifies to it. As Sgt. Daniel Kanipe recalled: "I next went along the line of dead bodies toward the river, and riding along the edge of the deep gully about 2,000 feet from where the monument now stands, I counted 28 bodies in the gulch." How these men came to be killed here and why no markers were placed here remain mysteries. Archeological excavations in 1984 failed to solve the riddle.

17 Custer Hill

The remnants of Custer's command gathered on the western slope of Battle Ridge at its northern end, just below the present monument. They shot their horses for breastworks and fought the "last stand" of history and legend. After the battle, Lt. Edward S. Godfrey, one of Reno's officers, counted 42 men here behind a barricade of 39 dead horses.

One of the bodies was Custer's. At what stage of the fighting he fell is not known. Some Indian accounts tell of a soldier in buckskin fitting Custer's description being shot at the ford at the mouth of Medicine Tail Coulee. Whatever happened, Custer's body was identified in the last stand group, just below the crest of the ridge. Next to him lay his brother Tom, mutilated almost beyond recognition. In contrast, Colonel Custer's remains escaped mutilation, prompting speculation that he had been spared out of respect. Most Indian accounts, however, indicate that the warriors recognized

Deep Ravine.

Custer Hill.

108

Custer National Cemetery.

no particular person among the soldiers. As the Oglala Low Dog remarked: "Everything was in confusion all the time of the fight. I did not see General Custer. I do not know who killed him. We did not know till the fight was over that he was the white chief."

Among the headstones in this group are those of George, Tom, and Boston Custer as well as other officers. On top of the hill stands the monument erected in 1881 bearing the names of all officers and soldiers killed in the battle. The remains of the slain troopers lay in a common grave around its base.

⑱ National Cemetery

Nearly 5,000 soldiers and their dependents are buried in Custer National Cemetery. Originally established to commemorate the dead of the battle, it was later expanded to receive veterans of all wars and their dependents. Interments include soldiers from the Indian Wars, the Spanish-American War, World Wars I and II, the Korean War, and Vietnam War. Major Reno, moved from elsewhere in 1973, and Lt. John J. Crittenden, who fell on Calhoun Hill, are also buried here. The cemetery has been officially closed since 1977.

Index

Italicized numbers indicate photo, illustration, or map.

☆GPO: 1987 — 181-413/60002 Reprint 1995

National Park Service

About the Author
Robert M. Utley is a former Chief Historian and Assistant Director of the National Park Service. He began his career in the Service at Little Bighorn Battlefield National Monument, where he served as historian from 1947-52. He is the author of numerous books and articles on military and Indian topics, including a two-volume history of the U.S. Army and the Indian, *Frontiersmen in Blue*, and *Frontier Regulars*. Among his recent books is *Cavalier in Buckskin: George Armstrong Custer and the Western Military Tradition* and *The Lance and the Shield: The Life and Times of Sitting Bull.*

Acknowledgments
The foregoing narrative owes a large debt to the work of Dr. John S. Gray, whose *Centennial Campaign: The Sioux War of 1876* (Fort Collins, Colo.: Old Army Press, 1976) incorporates some of the most penetrating and creative research, analysis, and interpretation yet to appear. Also contributing heavily were Jerome A. Greene, *Evidence and the Custer Enigma: A Reconstruction of Indian-Military History*, published by the Kansas City Posse of the Westerners in 1973; and Richard G. Hardoff, *Markers, Artifacts and Indian Testimony: Preliminary Findings on the Custer Battle*, published in 1985 by Don Horn Publications. Recognition is due several officers and members of the Little Big Horn Associates for their help: W. Donald Horn, Brian C. Pohanka, John M. Carroll, and W. Boyes.

Part 3, the guide to Little Bighorn Battlefield, is the work of Neil C. Mangum, historian at Little Bighorn Battlefield National Monument when this publication was prepared. Mangum also contributed substantially to all other parts of this work.